I0411903

1. No law protects you against visa-discrimination in USA.

2. EEOC and other agencies are merely a joke.

3. Judges in courts are biased towards their own people and treat foreigners as trash.

4. Lawyers will rip you apart, who could pay $500 per hour in lawyer's fee.

5. Universities have top lawyers and you don't stand a chance against them.

6. You would spend thousands of dollars and many years to earn a degree to realize that you can't get a job in the USA.

7. If you don't agree then give it a shot. Many students who did not agree with me are now suffering and asking for my advise.

I decided to write this book after my own experience of higher studies in the United States of America. I came to United States from India in 2007.

Here are the events:

January 2008- Joined the PhD Program in Biochemistry at the University of Texas Health Science Center at San Antonio

January 11, 2011-Submitted Dissertation Proposal to the Committee (part of requirement of the PhD program)

May 2, 2011- Departmental Seminar presented in regard to dissertation proposal after verbal approval from committee

August 2, 2011- Requested committee to approve the dissertation proposal-No Response

August 26, 2011- Requested committee second time to approve the proposal- No Response

October 18, 2011- Sent a third reminder and also made aware that I was getting late in submitting my proposal to the Chair of graduate studies, Dr. Neal C. Robinson- Got no response again

December 6, 2011- Informed Dr. Neal C. Robinson that the committee is not responding to his requests- No response from Dr. Robinson either.

December, 2011 and January 17, 2012- My supervisor told me that he could get my visa cancelled and send me back to India, if I did not follow my supervisor's guidelines on work schedule. It included working overtime, on weekends and also during Christmas holidays.

January 20, 2012- I was placed on academic probation for failure to submit dissertation proposal (which I had already submitted) and an unsatisfactory grade in my research performance (even though I had met the requirements set in the policy handbook for that semester).

February 24, 2012- I was issued another letter by Dr. Robinson asking me to finish all the aims of my dissertation in 1 semester or else face dismissal; however I had approximately 4 more semesters to finish this work.

February 24, 2012- I wrote an e-mail to Dr. Robinson to accept my e-mail as my resignation from the program if their practice was to continue.

February 28, 2012- Complained to Dean about the harassment I was facing

February 29, 2012- Dr. Robinson wrote an e-mail, telling me that I have not contacted him regarding these issues (however Dr. Robinson knew from December 6, 2011 about these issues).

March 8, 2012- I contacted Dean and asked him if any investigation of my complaint was being planned- No response from Dean

March 12, 2012- Associate Dean wrote an e-mail to me, telling me that I have already resigned from the program on February 24, 2012, so he did not understand the purpose of my e-mails after February 24, 2012. He also wrote that if I did not meet with him by March 21, 2012 then he will officially start the paperwork of my resignation. I never went to meet with him.

March 12, 2012- Chairman of my department wrote an e-mail to associate dean and sent a copy to me. He wrote that my resignation be accepted immediately and my university support (salary) be terminated immediately. Also, I would not be allowed to publish my recent research work under the university's name.

September 6, 2012- I was dismissed from the university

despite my resigning from the program 6 months prior to dismissal.

October 29, 2013- I contacted Dean to change my dismissal to resignation. I realized in October 2013 that I would need to send transcripts from all the schools attended including the school from where I have not received a degree. I was of this impression that a transcript is required only from the schools from where a degree is earned.

November 14, 2013- I re-contacted Dean since I did not get a response from him.

November 21, 2013- He suggested me to talk to the Vice president.

November 24, 2013- I contacted Vice President

December 5, 2013- I met with Vice President to request him to change my dismissal into resignation

December 15, 2013- I received a letter from Vice President stating that the university will not change my dismissal into a resignation and my transcripts will reflect dismissal.

So, I was a PhD student in the Department of Biochemistry at the University of Texas Health Science Center at San Antonio. My supervisor's name was Philip Serwer. Students who are pursuing PhD know that they are required to submit a dissertation proposal as part of the program. I submitted it to my committee. The committee never approved it, but rather placed me on probation saying that I have failed to submit my dissertation proposal. It was a lie, since I did submit them the proposal. They gave me a whole list of aims and asked me to finish it 3 months or face dismissal. That is called black-mailing.

I offered resignation. They did not accept my resignation for 6 months even after my repeated requests but rather dismissed me from the program and wrote this information on my educational transcript. This is 'my way or the highway' at its best.

The story does not end here. I thought United States had one of the best legal systems in the world. Well, I was wrong. My case was dismissed from lower to higher courts. The bias of the judges could be clearly seen in the rulings that they wrote.

So, after spending 7 years and thousands of dollars on legal battle, I have come to the conclusion that this country will not give you justice if you are treated as **slaves** here. Students are hired from other countries. They make progress in the programs and when it comes time to give the degrees, professors' black-mail them. So, one could either yield to their demands which could involve working up to 16 hours a day or seek legal help. The legal battle is a certain loss because courts favor its own people here. They are politically oriented not legally.

Many students have tried to fight discrimination in US universities and have failed miserably. I know a girl who came from India. I told her the bull-shit system of the university. She did not believe me. She got all A grades and was very happy until time came to choose her laboratory. She rotated in 4 labs and none of them had funding. She talked to the Dean and told him that she rotated based on a list in which names of the faculty members with funding was given. The Dean did not do anything about it. Eventually, she was issued a letter stating that she failed to find a mentor and so she was dismissed.

I know it is height of crap but this is how many universities in USA work. If a supervisor tells you that you have to do this or your visa would be terminated and you would be deported, there is nothing you could do about it. The agencies like EEOC are nothing more than a joke. If you file a complaint with them, they will most probably dismiss it. They will only take 1 in a 10000 case just to show that they work. If you decide to go to court, be prepared to have your case dismissed by a biased judge. My own case was thrown out because my case ended up in the court of Royce C. Lamberth, a conservative judge who does not like foreign faces in this country. I appealed to the 5th circuit, where my appeal was denied in a very aggressive and biased manner of writing by judges Patrick Higginbotham, Edith Jones and Stephen Higginson. Edith Jones had been under controversy for her racial remarks. So, how could one expect justice in a country where people who are supposed to serve justice are themselves possibly racists?

Why would one spend thousands of dollars to come to this country just to get oneself fucked in the ass? You need to ask this before deciding to take hard earned money of your parents.

Type my name as Saurav Pathria in Google and you will find some documents of my case with the university.

I am also enclosing some of correspondence with my committee members whose names were:

1. Philip Serwer
2. Stephen Hardies
3. Susan Weintraub
4. William Haldenwang

Other individuals who acted with utmost disregard were:

5. David Weiss was the Dean
6. Larry Barnes was Associate Dean
7. Neal Robinson was Chair of Graduate Committee
8. Bruce Nicholson was Chair of Biochemistry
9. Micheal Gargano was Vice President of the University

Following are mixed documents. Some documents are from my mentors in India. My transcript from University of Texas shows that I was given two successive Un-satisfactory grades despite the fact that I was not even attending the semester for which I was given unsatisfactory grade since I had already resigned because of slave-like treatment. Some documents below are from my time at the university and during the time of legal battle. The documents are not arranged by date because some events ran simultaneously but separately.

SCHOOL OF MEDICINE
UT HEALTH SCIENCE CENTER
SAN ANTONIO

University : Home | Calendar | Maps
WE MAKE LIVES BETTER

Site University Enter Keywords [Search]

Home
People
Graduate Programs
Seminars
Directories
Library
UT Conversano
Biochemistry Service Desk
Biochemistry Administration

Contact Info

Phone: (210) 567-3770
Fax: (210) 567-6595

News

Department News
Research Breakthroughs
Student / Post Doctoral
Achievements
New Additions
Student IMGP Compensation

Calendar

Seminar Schedule

SEMINAR SCHEDULE

Department of Biochemistry

Date	Time	Room	Notes
	Spring 2011		
Fri, Jan 21	Dr. Bettie Sue Masters, Department of Biochemistry, UTHSCSA; Biochemistry and Biology of Cytochrome P450 Reductase: From Test Tube to Mouse Model		
	12:00-1:00 pm	409-410L (Medical School Bldg.)	
Fri, Jan 28	POSTPONED: Dr. Susan Weintraub, Department of Biochemistry, UTHSCSA!		
			POSTPONED to Feb. 18 due to campus closure.
Fri, Feb 11	Dr. Randy Strong, Department of Pharmacology and Barshop Center, UTHSCSA; Pharmacological Intervention in the Aging Process		
	12:00-1:00 pm	409-410L (Medical School Bldg.)	Hosted by: Dr. John C. Lee
Fri, Feb 18	Dr. Susan Weintraub, Professor, Department of Biochemistry, UTHSCSA; Identification and Characterization of Proteins by Mass Spectrometry: What Can You Learn and What Can You Believe?		
	12:00-1:00 pm	409-410L (Medical School Bldg.)	Hosted by: Dr. Bruce J. Nicholson.
Fri, Feb 25	Dr. John Clark, Dept. of Biological Structure, Univ. of Washington at Seattle; Human alphaB crystallin, Neurodegeneration and Lens Opacification		
	12:00-1:00 pm	409-410L (Medical School Bldg.)	Hosted by: Dr. Jean X. Jiang
Mon, Mar 7	Qian Shi, Comprehensive Biochemistry Student Review; Ubiquitin and Human Diseases		
	1:00 – 2:00 p.m	409-410L (Medical School Bldg.)	Qian's Mentor and Professor: Dr. Jean X. Jiang.
Fri, Mar 11	Dr. Alan Cowman, Div. Head, Infection and Immunity, Walter and Eliza Hall Institute, Australia; Moving in and Renovating: Remodeling of the Human Erythrocyte by the Malaria Parasite		
	12:00-1:00 pm	409-410L (Medical School Bldg.)	Hosted by: Dr. Philip LoVerde
Fri, Mar 18	Dr. Richard Cerione, Goldwin Smith Professor, Dept. of Molecular Medicine, College of Veterinary Medicine, Cornell University; Cdc42: Some Obvious and Not So Obvious Roles in Biology		
	12:00-1:00 pm	409-410L (Medical School Bldg.)	Hosted by Dr. Bruce J. Nicholson
Fri, Mar 25	Dr. David Fulton, Assoc. Professor, Vascular Biology Ctr. & Pharmacology, Medical College of Georgia; Control of Reactive Species production by Molecular Chaperones		
	12:00-1:00 pm	409-410L (Medical School Bldg.)	Hosted by: Dr. Reto Asmis
Tue, Mar 29	Jiayan Guo, Comprehensive Biochemistry Student Review.; Disorders of Neuronal Migration Caused by Filamin A, LIS1, and Doublecortin in the Development of Cerebral Cortex		

	2:00 – 3:00 pm	409-410L (Medical School Bldg.)	Jiayan's Mentor and Professor: Dr. Richard F. Ludueña Àã§ää

Fri, Apr 1 Dr. Hector Viadiu, Dept. of Chemistry and Biochemistry, Univ. of California at San Diego; Structural Studies on p53 Regulation

	12:00-1:00 pm	409-410L (Medical School Bldg.)	Hosted by: Dr. Dmitri Ivanov

Mon, Apr 11 Jiayan Guo, Doctoral Dissertation Defense, Department of Biochemistry, UTHSCSA; The Roles of Beta Tubulin Isotypes in Neurons

	9:00-10:00 am	409-410L (Medical School Bldg.)	Jiayan's Mentor and Professor: Dr. Richard F. Ludueña.

Wed, Apr 20 Rohit Kulkarni, M.D., Ph.D., Department of Cell Biology, Joslin Diabetes Center, Harvard Medical School.; Role of Growth Factor Signaling in the Regulation of Proinsulin Processing and Endoplasmic Reticulum Stress in Pancreatic Beta Cells

	12:00-1:00 pm	4.434.T (Dental School Bldg.)	Hosted by Dr. Martin Adamo. Sponsored by the Biochemistry Dept. and the MD/PhD Program

Fri, Apr 29 Dr. Daniel Leahy, Dept. of Biophysics and biophysical Chemistry, Johns Hopkins Univ. School of Medicine, Structural Basis for EGFR/ErbB Signaling and ErbB-targeted Therapies

	12:00-1:00 pm	409-410L (Medical School Bldg.)	Hosted by: Dr. Chongwoo Kim

Mon, May 2 Saurav Pathria, Dissertation Proposal Seminar.; Genetic Analysis of Assembly-Associated Transitions of the Major Capsid Protein, gp10A, of Phage T3

	3:00-4:00 pm	409-410L (Medical School Bldg.)	Saurav's Mentor and Professor: Dr. Philip Serwer; PLEASE NOTE THE UNUSUAL DATE AND TIME OF THIS PRESENTATION.

Fri, May 6 Dr. Yun-Xing Wang, Head, Protein-Nucleic Acid Interactions Section, Structural Biophysics laboratory, NCI; How Small Can be Global: Application of Small Angle X-ray Scattering to Structural Biology Studies

	12:00-1:00 pm	409-410L (Medical School Bldg.)	Hosted by: Dr. Andrew P. Hinck

Fri, May 20 Dr. Thomas Biederer, Department of Molecular Biophysics and Biochemistry, Yale University; More Than Synaptic Glue: Control of Synapse Structure and Function by Trans-Synaptic Adhesion

	12:00-1:00 pm	409-410L (Medical School Bldg.)	Hosted by: Dr. Eileen M. Lafer Sponsored by the Department of Biochemistry and SALSI.

Mon, Jun 27 Rugmani Padmanabhan, Comprehensive Biochemistry Student Review.; Target of Rapamycin: Mechanism of Action & Role in Diseases

	3:00-4:00 pm	409-410L (Medical School Bldg.)	Rugmani's Mentor and Professor: Dr. Jean X. Jiang.

Tue, Jul 19 Qian Shi, Doctoral Dissertation Defense, Department of Biochemistry, UTHSCSA; Mechanistic Study of Connexin 50 in Promotion of Lens Cell Differentiation, a Gap Junction Independent Role

	9:30-10:30 am	444-445B	Qian's Mentor and Professor: Dr. Jean X. Jiang.

Tue, Jul 19 Dr. A. Sue Menko, Professor Department of Pathology, Anatomy and Cell Biology, Thomas Jefferson University; Novel Paradigms of Wound Healing and Fibrosis Revealed in a Lens Injury Model

	3:00-4:00 pm	444-445B (Medical School Bldg.)	Hosted by: Dr. Jean X. Jiang

Wed, Jul 27 Nidhi Batra, Comprehensive Biochemistry Student Review.; Integrin Signaling and Cancer: Biological Implications and Therapeutics

WE MAKE LIVES BETTER

UT HEALTH SCIENCE CENTER™

DEPARTMENT OF BIOCHEMISTRY
Mail Code 7760
7703 Floyd Curl Drive   Office (210) 567-3754
San Antonio, TX 78229-3900   FAX   (210) 567-659

January 20, 2012

Mr. Saurav Pathria
Graduate Student
Department of Biochemistry
Univ. Texas Health Science Center
San Antonio, TX 78229

RE: Academic Probation in the Biochemistry Ph.D. Program

Dear Saurav,

I must inform you that as of today you are formally on academic probation in the Biochemistry Ph.D.
graduate program. You have been placed on probation because of two deficiencies in your academic
performance: 1) you have failed to submit your committee approved Ph.D. proposal by the required
submission date; and 2) you have received a grade of Unsatisfactory (U) in BIOC 6097 (Research). If
these deficiencies remain at the end of Spring Semester, 2012, your academic progress in the
Biochemistry Ph.D. Program will be reviewed by the Biochemistry Committee on Graduate Studies
(COGS). If COGS judges that your academic progress remains unsatisfactory, you will be subject to
dismissal from the Biochemistry Ph.D. Program.

If you have any questions regarding these academic requirements, please refer to the Policy Handbook for
the Biochemistry Graduate Program which clearly states:

1. A student is placed on academic probation for failure to meet any of the requirements of the
   program.
2. "If a student did not submit the specified documents to COGS by the end of the sixth semester, the
   student must have obtained the approval of COGS for a postponement. The student should submit a
   letter to the Graduate Advisor stating the reason for seeking the postponement and stating a proposed
   date for submission of the documents. The letter must be signed by all members of the proposed
   Dissertation Supervising Committee, except the external examiner, to indicate their agreement with
   the reason for seeking a postponement."
3. A student who fails to meet the probationary requirements, or who fails to satisfy a second
   requirement while on probation is subject to dismissal from the Ph.D. program.

Sincerely,

Neal C. Robinson, Ph.D.
Professor of Biochemistry
Chair of Biochemistry COGS

WE MAKE LIVES BETTER
UT HEALTH SCIENCE CENTER™

DEPARTMENT OF BIOCHEMISTRY
Mail Code 7760
7703 Floyd Curl Drive   Office (210) 567-3754
San Antonio, TX 78229-3900   FAX   (210) 567-659

January 20, 2012

Mr. Saurav Pathria
Graduate Student, Department of Biochemistry
University of Texas Health Science Center
San Antonio, TX 78229

RE: Academic Probation in the Biochemistry Ph.D. Program

Dear Saurav,

On January 20th of this year, I informed that you were being placed on academic probation based upon your academic deficiencies in the Biochemistry Ph.D. graduate program. I must remind you once again that unless you satisfactorily address these deficiencies by the end of Spring Semester, 2012, your graduate status in the Biochemistry Ph.D. Program will be reviewed by the Biochemistry Committee on Graduate Studies (COGS). If COGS judges that your academic progress remains unsatisfactory, you will be subject to dismissal from the Biochemistry Ph.D. Program.

To help you understand the seriousness of these problems, and to assist you in removing your probationary status, your dissertation committee has decided that removal from probationary status is contingent on the following.

1. First, you must submit the signed dissertation committee evaluation forms to COGS for Fall Semester, 2011.

2. Second, you must make sufficient progress in the laboratory to receive a grade of at least satisfactory from your dissertation supervising committee for Spring Semester, 2012. The committee members expect performance at the level of past graduate students of similar experience. Specifically, this requirement means (a) construction of at least two cloned mutants of gene 10 for each of three targeted regions, (b) verification of mutant status by sequencing each of the cloned genes, (c) demonstration of assembly capacity of mutant gp10, either by a valid complementation assay or by recovery of a recombinant phage and verifying mutant status by sequencing, (d) determination of propagation characteristics and (e) obtaining of a preliminary phenotype, non-denaturing gel analysis being sufficient. It should be evident what amount of mutant virions can be produced and that these amounts are sufficient to support proposed characterization experiments under (3).

3. Finally, you must complete your dissertation proposal and have it approved by his supervising committee. The Committee expects the proposal to be rewritten to contain at least two specific aims, each of which specifies characterization of mutants sufficient to confirm or reject a hypothesis about the function of the capsid protein, gp10. Each proposed experiment should be described in sufficient detail for feasibility to be apparent to the Committee. For example, reference should be made to preliminary experiments that indicate that sufficient amounts of virions can be made. Preliminary results should be presented. These results should be in Figure format and should illustrate what differences are expected between mutant and wild type, as predicted by the hypotheses. The experiments proposed should have discriminatory power to distinguish between insufficient or mistimed protein production, folding deficiency and assembly defects. The procedure for quantification should be indicated.

Sincerely,

Neal C. Robinson, Ph.D.
Professor of Biochemistry
Chair of Biochemistry COGS

| Search Mail | Search Web | saurav_pa... | Profile ∨ Go | Sign Out | Home

HealthAndStyleMag.com   Losing your Hair?   Sponsored

RE: Transcript Issues   Thursday, December 5, 2013 12:45 AM

From: "Rodriguez Sandra J" <RODRIGUEZSJ@uthscsa.edu>

To: "saurav pathria" <saurav_pathria@yahoo.com>

Cc: "Salas Ashley Anne" <salasaa@uthscsa.edu> "Rodriguez Sandra J" <RODRIGUEZSJ@uthscsa.edu>

Good afternoon Saurav,
Dr. Gargano's VP for AFSA office is located in the Academic and Administration building. I have advised the guard stationed at the front reception area and she will advise me of your arrival. I will meet you at the elevators on the 4th floor of the AAB and I will walk you to Dr. Gargano's office located in the SHP Dean's office.

Please let me know if you have additional questions or concerns.

Have a good afternoon,
Sandra

-----Original Message-----
From: saurav pathria [mailto:saurav_pathria@yahoo.com]
Sent: Wednesday, December 04, 2013 11:44 AM
To: Rodriguez, Sandra J
Cc: Gargano, Michael; Rodriguez, Sandra J; Salas, Ashley Anne
Subject: RE: Transcript Issues

Hello Sandra,

I am available for a meeting tomorrow (December 5th, 12-1pm). Please let me know the room number and the location.

Thank you.
Saurav Pathria

On Wed, 12/4/13, Rodriguez, Sandra J <RODRIGUEZSJ@uthscsa.edu> wrote:

Subject: RE: Transcript Issues
To: "saurav pathria" <saurav_pathria@yahoo.com>
Cc: "Gargano, Michael" <Gargano@uthscsa.edu>, "Rodriguez, Sandra J" <RODRIGUEZSJ@uthscsa.edu>, "Salas, Ashley Anne" <salasaa@uthscsa.edu>
Date: Wednesday, December 4, 2013, 8:58 PM

Good morning Saurav.
Please see attached email response.

Thank you.
Sandra

-----Original Message-----
From: saurav pathria [mailto:saurav_pathria@yahoo.com]

Sent: Wednesday, December 04, 2013 8:56 AM
To: Rodriguez, Sandra J
Cc: Gargano, Michael
Subject: RE: Transcript Issues

Hello Sandra,

Dr. Gargano has asked me to contact you to set a time schedule for a meeting with him.

I am available this week.

Thank you.
Saurav Pathria

On Wed, 12/4/13, Gargano, Michael <Gargano@uthscsa.edu> wrote:

Subject: RE: Transcript Issues
To: "saurav pathria" <saurav_pathria@yahoo.com>, Rodriguez, Sandra J <RODRIGUEZSJ@uthscsa.edu>
Cc: "Weiss, David" <weissd@uthscsa.edu>

		2:00-3:00 pm	444-445B (Medical School Bldg.)	Nidhi's Mentor and Professor: Dr. Jean X. Jiang.
Thu, Aug 11	Pramod Gowda, Comprehensive Biochemistry Student Review; Molecular Mechanism of Metastasis and Identification of Metastasis Suppressor Genes			
		2:00 - 3:00 pm	409-410L (Medical School Bldg.)	Pramod Gowda's Mentor and Professor: Dr. Donald McEwen.
Tue, Aug 16	Chi Fung Lee, Comprehensive Biochemistry Student Review; Mitochondrial Dynamics: Biochemistry and Pathology			
		2:00-3:00 pm	409-410L (Medical School Bldg.)	Chi Fung Lee's Mentor and Professor: Dr. Peter Asins).

Contact the Dept.
Updated: 11/07/2008
Copyright © 2008
The University of Texas Health Science
Center at San Antonio

Department of Biochemistry | The University of Texas Health Science Center

Department of Biochemistry | School of Medicine | Graduate School of Biomedical Sciences |
UT Health Science Center | Briscoe Library | Inside UTHSCSA

EEOC Form 5 (11/09)

CHARGE OF DISCRIMINATION		Charge Presented To:	Agency(ies) Charge No(s):
This form is affected by the Privacy Act of 1974. See enclosed Privacy Act Statement and other information before completing this form.		☐ FEPA	
		☒ EEOC	. 451-2012-01175

Texas Workforce Commission Civil Rights Division	and EEOC
State or local Agency, if any	

Name (indicate Mr., Ms., Mrs.)	Home Phone (Incl. Area Code)	Date of Birth
Mr. Saurav Pathria	(614) 264-6702	02-28-1981

Street Address	City, State and ZIP Code	
8525 Floyd Curl Drive, Apt. 504, San Antonio, TX 78240		

Named is the Employer, Labor Organization, Employment Agency, Apprenticeship Committee, or State or Local Government Agency That I Believe Discriminated Against Me or Others. (If more than two, list under PARTICULARS below.)

Name	No. Employees, Members	Phone No. (Include Area Code)
UTHSC AT SAN ANTONIO	500 or More	

Street Address	City, State and ZIP Code		
7703 Floyd Curl Drive, San Antonio, TX 78229			

Name	No. Employees, Members	Phone No. (Include Area Code)

Street Address	City, State and ZIP Code	

DISCRIMINATION BASED ON (Check appropriate box(es).)

☐ RACE ☐ COLOR ☐ SEX ☐ RELIGION ☒ NATIONAL ORIGIN

☐ RETALIATION ☐ AGE ☐ DISABILITY ☐ GENETIC INFORMATION

☐ OTHER (Specify)

DATE(S) DISCRIMINATION TOOK PLACE
Earliest 01-20-2012   Latest 03-09-2012

☒ CONTINUING ACTION

THE PARTICULARS ARE (If additional paper is needed, attach extra sheet(s)):

On or about January 20, 2012 I was placed on probation by Dr. Philip Serwer and Dr. Neal Robinson for not complying with established requirements. I have accomplished more than other teaching assistants and complied with directions and policies. Dr. Neal is well aware I have submitted documents and done what was asked of me in a timely manner, but the committee responsible for processing my papers is holding it up and they have not given me any feedback or directions on what if any other actions I'm supposed to do.

Dr. Serwer uses the fact I am from India to harass and intimidate me by telling me I need to work as much as he wants me to, when he wants me to because he has the power to cancel my visa and send me back to India. I believe Dr. Serwer treats me disparately because I am from India.

I have asked the Dean for assistance, but I have not heard back from him. Dr. Serwer continues to harass and intimidate me.

I believe that I am being discriminated against and subjected to a hostile work environment based on my national origin, India in violation of Title VII of the Civil Rights Act of 1964, as amended.

I want this charge filed with both the EEOC and the State or local Agency, if any. I will advise the agencies if I change my address or phone number and I will cooperate fully with them in the processing of my charge in accordance with their procedures.	NOTARY – When necessary for State and Local Agency Requirements
I declare under penalty of perjury that the above is true and correct.	I swear or affirm that I have read the above charge and that it is true to the best of my knowledge, information and belief. SIGNATURE OF COMPLAINANT
Mar 09, 2012	SUBSCRIBED AND SWORN TO BEFORE ME THIS DATE (month, day, year)
Date Charging Party Signature	

PRIVACY ACT STATEMENT: Under the Privacy Act of 1974, Pub. Law 93-579, authority to request personal data and its uses are:

1. FORM NUMBER/TITLE/DATE. EEOC Form 5, Charge of Discrimination (11/09).

2. AUTHORITY. 42 U.S.C. 2000e-5(b), 29 U.S.C. 211, 29 U.S.C. 626, 42 U.S.C. 12117, 42 U.S.C. 2000ff-6.

3. PRINCIPAL PURPOSES. The purposes of a charge, taken on this form or otherwise reduced to writing (whether later recorded on this form or not) are, as applicable under the EEOC anti-discrimination statutes (EEOC statutes), to preserve private suit rights under the EEOC statutes, to invoke the EEOC's jurisdiction and, where dual-filing or referral arrangements exist, to begin state or local proceedings.

4. ROUTINE USES. This form is used to provide facts that may establish the existence of matters covered by the EEOC statutes (and as applicable, other federal, state or local laws). Information given will be used by staff to guide its mediation and investigation efforts and, as applicable, to determine, conciliate and litigate claims of unlawful discrimination. This form may be presented to or disclosed to other federal, state or local agencies as appropriate or necessary in carrying out EEOC's functions. A copy of this charge will ordinarily be sent to the respondent organization against which the charge is made.

5. WHETHER DISCLOSURE IS MANDATORY; EFFECT OF NOT GIVING INFORMATION. Charges must be reduced to writing and should identify the charging and responding parties and the actions or policies complained of. Without a written charge, EEOC will ordinarily not act on the complaint. Charges under Title VII, the ADA or GINA must be sworn to or affirmed (either by using this form or by presenting a notarized statement or unsworn declaration under penalty of perjury); charges under the ADEA should ordinarily be signed. Charges may be clarified or amplified later by amendment. It is not mandatory that this form be used to make a charge.

NOTICE OF RIGHT TO REQUEST SUBSTANTIAL WEIGHT REVIEW

Charges filed at a state or local Fair Employment Practices Agency (FEPA) that dual-files charges with EEOC will ordinarily be handled first by the FEPA. Some charges filed at EEOC may also be first handled by a FEPA under worksharing agreements. You will be told which agency will handle your charge. When the FEPA is the first to handle the charge, it will notify you of its final resolution of the matter. Then, if you wish EEOC to give Substantial Weight Review to the FEPA's final findings, you must ask us in writing to do so within 15 days of your receipt of its findings. Otherwise, we will ordinarily adopt the FEPA's finding and close our file on the charge.

NOTICE OF NON-RETALIATION REQUIREMENTS

Please notify EEOC or the state or local agency where you filed your charge if retaliation is taken against you or others who oppose discrimination or cooperate in any investigation or lawsuit concerning this charge. Under Section 704(a) of Title VII, Section 4(d) of the ADEA, Section 503(a) of the ADA and Section 207(f) of GINA, it is unlawful for an employer to discriminate against present or former employees or job applicants, for an employment agency to discriminate against anyone, or for a union to discriminate against its members or membership applicants, because they have opposed any practice made unlawful by the statutes, or because they have made a charge, testified, assisted, or participated in any manner in an investigation, proceeding, or hearing under the laws. The Equal Pay Act has similar provisions and Section 503(b) of the ADA prohibits coercion, intimidation, threats or interference with anyone for exercising or enjoying, or aiding or encouraging others in their exercise or enjoyment of, rights under the Act.

U.S. Equal Employment Opportunity Commission
San Antonio Field Office

5410 Fredericksburg Rd
Suite 200
San Antonio, TX 78229
(210) 281-2550
TTY (210) 281-7610
Fax: (210) 281-7690

Respondent: UTHSC AT SAN ANTONIO
EEOC Charge No.: 451-2012-01175
FEPA Charge No.:

March 9, 2012

Saurav Pathria
8525 Floyd Curl Drive, Apt. 504
San Antonio, TX 78240

Dear Mr. Pathria:

This is with reference to your recent written correspondence or intake questionnaire in which you alleged employment discrimination by the above-named respondent. The information provided indicates that the matter complained of is subject to the statute(s) checked off below:

[X]   Title VII of the Civil Rights Act of 1964 (Title VII)

[ ]   The Age Discrimination in Employment Act (ADEA)

[ ]   The Americans with Disabilities Act (ADA)

[ ]   The Equal Pay Act (EPA)

[ ]   The Genetic Information Nondiscrimination Act (GINA)

The attached EEOC Form 5, Charge of Discrimination, is a summary of your claims based on the information you provided. Because the document that you submitted to us constitutes a charge of employment discrimination, we have complied with the law and notified the employer that you filed a charge. Before we investigate your charge, however, you must sign and return the enclosed Form.

To enable proper handling of this action by the Commission you should:

(1) Review the enclosed charge form and make corrections.

(2) Sign and date the charge in the bottom left hand block where I have made an "X". For purposes of meeting the deadline for filing a charge, the date of your original signed document will be retained as the original filling date.

(3) Return the signed charge to this office.

Before we initiate an investigation, we must receive your signed Charge of Discrimination (EEOC Form 5). Please sign and return the charge within thirty (30) days from the date of this letter. Under EEOC procedures, if we do not hear from you within 30 days or receive your signed charge within 30 days, we are authorized to dismiss your charge and issue you a right to sue letter allowing you to pursue the matter in federal court. Please be aware that after we receive your signed Form 5, the EEOC will send a copy of the charge to Texas Workforce Commission Civil Rights Division 101 East 15th St Room 144T Austin, TX 78778 as required by our procedures. If that agency processes the charge, it may require the charge to be signed before a notary public or an agency official. The agency will then investigate and resolve the charge under their statute.

Please use the "EEOC Charge No." listed at the top of this letter whenever you call us about this charge. Please also notify this office of any change in address or of any prolonged absence from home. Failure to cooperate in this matter may lead to dismissal of the charge.

Please also read the enclosed brochure, "What You Should Know Before You File A Charge With EEOC," for answers to frequently asked questions about employee rights and the EEOC process. If you have any questions, please call me at the number listed below. If you have to call long distance, please call collect.

Sincerely,

George Hamilton
Investigator
(210) 281-7662

Office Hours: Monday – Friday, 8:30 a.m. - 5:00 p.m.
www.eeoc.gov

Enclosure(s)
    Copy of EEOC Form 5, Charge of Discrimination
    Copy of EEOC Uniform Brochure, "What You Should Know Before You File A Charge With EEOC."

U.S. EQUAL EMPLOYMENT OPPORTUNITY COMMISSION
San Antonio Field Office

5410 Fredericksburg Road, Suite 200
San Antonio, TX 78229-3555
Intake Information Group: (800) 669-4000
Intake Information Group TTY: (800) 669-6820
San Antonio Status Line: (866) 408-8075
San Antonio Direct Dial: (210) 281-2550
FAX (210) 281-2522

CHARGING PARTY
INVITATION TO MEDIATE

DATE: *9 Mar, 12*

CHARGING PARTY: *Saurav Pathria*

CHARGE NUMBER: *451-2012-01175*

The Equal Employment Opportunity Commission (EEOC) has determined that your charge is eligible for mediation. Please review the attached pamphlet, *"Mediation—What You Need To Know And Why You Should Try It"*, and read how mediation can work for you. We would like for you to try and benefit from mediation!

Please check one of the following options and fill out your contact information in the box below. Lastly, return this INVITATION TO MEDIATE form to our MEDIATION STAFF within 20 days via mail to the address above or FAX to (210) 281-2512

OPTION #1: _____ YES, I WILL PARTICIPATE IN EEOC MEDIATION

OPTION #2: _____ I WOULD LIKE ADDITIONAL INFORMATION
ABOUT MEDIATION   *I do not want to*
Please complete the box regardless of the option selected: *mediate.*

Name: _____	Address: _____
City/State/Zip: _____	Phone: _____
Fax Number: _____	Cell Number: _____
Email: _____	
If you have representation, please provide the following information:	
Representative's Name: _____	Phone: _____
Representative's Address: _____	
Representative's City/State/Zip: _____	Fax: _____

U.S. EQUAL EMPLOYMENT OPPORTUNITY COMMISSION
San Antonio Field Office

5410 Fredericksburg Road, Suite 200
San Antonio, TX 78229-3555
San Antonio Status Line: (866) 408-8075
TTY (210) 281-7610
FAX (210) 281-7690

Dallas District
Dallas District Office
San Antonio Field Office
El Paso Area Office

My organization is an equal employment opportunity employer...

Almost everyone says they're for equal opportunity. Many of us believe we are truly committed to the principle. So why is equal opportunity so evasive in many of America's workplaces? Most of our organizational diversity is at lower levels. We all have ideas about impediments, but a major impediment may be between our ears!

Scientists know that, for a variety of reasons, people may not say what's on their minds. Notwithstanding our integrity and other ethical standards, there can be social, economic and other consequences for truth or for speaking our mind. Also, did you ever consider that you may not even know what's on your mind? Are you unconsciously hiding something from yourself? Try the *Implicit Association Tests*—they measure implicit attitudes and beliefs you may be unwilling or unable to acknowledge. Get your spouse, children, nieces, nephews and friends to try the tests—a fun, educational growth experience!

Go to: https://implicit.harvard.edu/implicit// and try...

Race IAT   **Do most Americans have an automatic preference for white over black?**

Skin-Tone IAT   **Is there an automatic preference for light-skin over dark-skin?**

Sex-Career IAT   **Reveals a relative link between family and females and between career and males.**

Age IAT   **Do you have an automatic preference for young over old?**

Saurav Pathria

go to ...   - ⊗

| Search | Enroll | My Academics |

My Advisors

Academic Program   Doctor of Philosophy
Major   PhD in Biochemistry

Notify	Advisor Name
☐	Peter Hart
☐	Guthie Hua
☐	Reed Solomon
☐	James Stone

Notify Selected Advisors   Notify All Advisors

Search   Enroll   My Academics

go to ...   - ⊗

Grades, Reporting Grades

Grading standards, symbols, grade point scales, GPA determinations, and other considerations regarding the quality of work of students are the prerogative of the faculty of the programs, as are issues of promotion and advancement.

Posting of Grades

Course grades of individual students may not be posted or made available in any public manner by name, initials, social security number, unique assigned student identification number, or other personal identifier except when the student has signed an authorization.

Before a student's grade can be posted, he/she will be asked to sign a consent form and be assigned a random number as a personal identifier. Generally, each individual faculty member who posts grades will go through the procedure to obtain consent and assign a number. (Some course instructors do not post grades.) In some schools, consent forms are processed by the Dean's Office. It is a student's right to decline to sign a consent form, in which case the student's grades will not be posted.

View Grades

Students may view their grades through Inside UTHSCSA.

GRADUATE SCHOOL OF BIOMEDICAL SCIENCES
UT HEALTH SCIENCE CENTER®
SAN ANTONIO

NOTIFICATION OF ADMISSION TO CANDIDACY

TO: __Saurav Pathria__
   Name of Student

I am pleased to inform you that the petition for your admission to candidacy for the
degree of:

[ ] Master of Science

[X] Doctor of Philosophy

in the field of:

__Biochemistry__
Graduate Program

_____
IMGP Track (if applicable)

has been approved, effective this date.

_____
Dean

____1/27/11____
Date

Distribution:
   Student (original)
   Registrar
   Chair of COGS
   Graduate Advisor
   Graduate School Office

GSBS Form 36
(07/10)

WE MAKE LIVES BETTER
UT HEALTH SCIENCE CENTER®
SAN ANTONIO

February 16, 2012

To Whom It May Concern:

This letter confirms that **Saurav PATHRIA**, SEVIS ID: N0004780958; DOB: 28 February 1981, is a doctoral student in Biochemistry at the University of Texas Health Science Center at San Antonio. **Saurav PATHRIA** began the program on 07 January 2008 and is expected to complete the program by 31 August 2013. **Saurav PATHRIA** is currently in good standing and maintains the terms and conditions of F-1 visa status.

If there are questions or additional information is required, please do not hesitate to contact me directly at Tel. 210-567-6241.

Sincerely,

Pauline Beazer James

Pauline P. Beazer James, M.Ed.
International Visitor Advisor
Office of International Services

WE MAKE LIVES BETTER
UT HEALTH SCIENCE CENTER®
SAN ANTONIO

December 10, 2013

Mr. Saurav Pathria
8525 Floyd Curl Drive
Apartment 504
San Antonio, Texas 78240

Dear Mr. Pathria,

As requested by your email communication on Sunday, November 24, 2013 and our personal meeting on Thursday, December 5, 2013, I have thoroughly reviewed the documents pertaining to your situation and listened attentively to your recollection of the matter.

I have considered all of the available information. I have reached a final decision that represents the University of Texas Health Science Center at San Antonio and the Graduate School for Biomedical Sciences. The conclusion is to uphold the decision of the Committee on Graduate Studies of the Biochemistry program in which you were formally dismissed from the program. Your Health Science Center transcript will reflect the dismissal.

Sincerely,

Dr. Michael Gargano
Vice President Academics, Faculty, and Student Affairs

CC:
Dean, Graduate School Biomedical Sciences
Director, Registrar Office

UT HEALTH SCIENCE CENTER®
OFFICE OF THE REGISTRAR

Student Clearance Form

This form should be completed and returned in person to the Office of the Registrar within 48 hours of the time it is initiated. A "HOLD" will be placed on official transcripts until the Registrar has been notified that the student's records have been cleared.

Section A: This section to be completed by Student.

Name: **Saurav Pathria**   HSC Badge # **0422831**   Phone: (___) _____

School: **GSB**   Program: **PhD**   Level: _____

Forwarding Address: _____ City: _____ State: _____ Zip _____

Type of Termination

_____ ADMINISTRATIVE LEAVE OF ABSENCE

_____ LEAVE OF ABSENCE: I understand I have been granted a leave of absence from school for a maximum of one calendar year. I realize I must contact the appropriate associate dean 30 days prior to re-enrolling and that I must register and pay fees at the appropriate time. If I decide not to return, I will formally notify the appropriate Associate Dean 30 days prior to the time I am expected to re-enroll.

ANTICIPATED DATE OF RETURN: _____

___✓___ VOLUNTARY WITHDRAWAL: I voluntarily withdraw from The UTHSCSA. I understand that I am leaving school permanently and that no mechanism exists through which I could be reinstated in the class I am presently leaving. I understand that if I wish to become a student again at this University, I must apply by the usual procedures and, in such event, would be considered for admission by the Admission Committee in competition with all other applications. My application would be reviewed without prejudice.

_____ DISMISSAL: I understand that I have been dismissed from UTHSCSA _____
                                                                    Name of School

_____ DID NOT RETURN

_____   _____
Signature of Student   Date

Section B. This section must be completed before Section C. This section is to be completed by the Department Chair (if applicable) and the Associate Dean of the School in which the student is enrolled.

I certify that the student named above is clearing under the category indicated.

The last official day this student attended class was: _____ (Month/Day/Year)

_____ _____ _____ _____
Signature of Department Chair (if applicable)   Date   Signature of Associate Dean   Date

Section C. The student must obtain signatures in each of the areas listed below and **RETURN THIS FORM TO THE OFFICE OF THE REGISTRAR. Complete Clearance Form in the order listed below.**

Clearance Areas	Authorized Signature/Date	Status	Reason for HOLD
Financial Aid •	_____ / _____	○ Clear **OR** ○ Hold	_____
Bursar (Student Accts)	_____ / _____	○ Clear **OR** ○ Hold	_____
Library	_____ / _____	○ Clear **OR** ○ Hold	_____
IID Labs Library Room 2.072	_____ / _____	○ Clear **OR** ○ Hold	_____
**SIM Lab D.S. Room 3.141T	_____ / _____	○ Clear **OR** ○ Hold	_____
***Outpatient Clinic Room 3 281R	_____ / _____	○ Clear **OR** ○ Hold	_____
****Curriculum Resources	_____ / _____	○ Clear **OR** ○ Hold	_____
University Police Traffic	_____ / _____	○ Clear **OR** ○ Hold	_____
University Police Keys	_____ / _____	○ Clear **OR** ○ Hold	_____

Note: Parking Permit and Student ID will be relinquished at this time.

Required **only** for: *MS 1, MS 2 & PA   **DS 1 & DS 2   ***DS 3 & DS 4   ****Undergraduate Nursing students

_____ _____
Registrar's Signature   Date

Revised 9/2012 ComputerForms

FINANCIAL AID COPY

Saurav Puthria

Name of Student

HSC Badge # D422831

_____

Address

(___)_____

Telephone

656

School

PhD

Program   Level

_____ /

Student's Last Official Class Day   Anticipated Date of Return

○ Leave of Absence   ○ Dismissal
● Withdrawal   ○ Did Not Return
Type of Termination

_____

Signature of Student

_____

Date

Favorites   Main Menu Self Service   Student Center

Saurav Pathria

| Search | Enroll | My Academics |

go to ...   ▼ ⊗

My Course History

Sort results by
Then by
sort

🔲 Taken   🔲 Transferred   🔲 In progress

Course	Description	Term	Grade	Units	Status
BIOC 0003	SCIENTIFIC WRITING	Fall 2009	S	1.00	☑
BIOC 0003	SCIENTIFIC WRITING	Fall 2010	S	1.00	☑
BIOC 0003	SCIENTIFIC WRITING	Fall 2011	S	1.00	☑
BIOC 5081	BIOCHEMICAL TECH LAB	Spring 2008	B	3.00	☑
BIOC 5081	BIOCHEMICAL TECH LAB	Summer 2008	A	1.00	☑
BIOC 5083	HYDRODYNAMIC METHODS	Spring 2008	B	2.00	☑
BIOC 5085	BIOPHYSICAL METHODS	Spring 2008	C	2.00	☑
BIOC 5085	BIOPHYSICAL METHODS	Spring 2010	B	2.00	☑
BIOC 5087	MOLECULAR BIOCHEMISTRY	Spring 2008	B	2.00	☑
BIOC 5091	SPECIAL TOPICS (MOLECULAR BIOCHEMISTRY)	Spring 2008	B	1.00	☑
BIOC 5010	SEMI EXT PRESSION	Spring 2008	B	2.00	☑
BIOC 5035	BIOL OF MULTICELLULAR COMPLEX	Fall 2009	A	3.00	☑
BIOC 6086	BIOC STUDENT REVIEW	Spring 2010	IP	1.00	☑
BIOC 6086	BIOC STUDENT REVIEW	Fall 2010	IP	1.00	☑
BIOC 6086	BIOC STUDENT REVIEW	Spring 2011	IP	1.00	☑
BIOC 6086	BIOC STUDENT REVIEW	Fall 2011	S	1.00	☑
BIOC 6071	SUPERVISED TEACHING	Fall 2009	S	1.00	☑
BIOC 6097	RESEARCH	Summer 2008	S	5.00	☑
BIOC 6097	RESEARCH	Fall 2008	S	1.00	☑
BIOC 6097	RESEARCH	Spring 2009	S	5.00	☑
BIOC 6097	RESEARCH	Summer 2009	S	6.00	☑
BIOC 6097	RESEARCH	Fall 2009	S	3.00	☑
BIOC 6097	RESEARCH	Spring 2010	S	6.00	☑
BIOC 6097	RESEARCH	Summer 2010	S	6.00	☑
BIOC 6097	RESEARCH	Fall 2010	S	7.00	☑
BIOC 6097	RESEARCH	Spring 2011	S	8.00	☑
BIOC 6097	RESEARCH	Summer 2011	S	6.00	☑
BIOC 6097	RESEARCH	Fall 2011	W	1.00	☑
BIOC 6097	RESEARCH	Spring 2012	V	9.00	☑
INTD 5000	PRINCIPLES OF BIOMEDICAL SCIENCES I	Fall 2008	B	6.00	☑
INTD 6002	ETHICS IN RESEARCH	Spring 2008	S	0.80	☑
INTD 6033	CELL SIGNALING MECHANISMS	Spring 2009	A	2.00	☑

Name   : Saurav Pathria
Student ID: P422051
Birthdate : 1981-12-28
Univ of Texas Health Science Center at San Antonio
7703 Floyd Curl Drive
San Antonio, TX 782283900
United States
Print Date : 2012-09-13
- - - - - Academic Program History - - - - -

Program   : Doctor of Philosophy
2007-10-06 : Active in Program
            2007-08-30 Biochemistry

2010-09-01 : Dismissed

- - - - - Beginning of Graduate School Graduate Record - - - - -
Sp 2008

BIOC	5091	BIOCHEMICAL TECH LAB	3.00	3.60 B	9.000
BIOC	5083	HYDRODYNAMIC METHODS	1.00	3.05 B	4.000
BIOC	5008	BIOPHYSICAL METHODS	1.00	0.05 C	
	Repeated : Grade Excluded from GPA		1.00	1.00 D	2.000
BIOC	5091	SPECIAL TOPICS	1.00	1.00 D	2.000
	Course Topic: Quantitative Biochemistry				
	Quantitative Biochemistry				
BIOC	6013	GENE EXPRESSION	3.00	3.50 B	8.000
INTD	0403	BASICS OF RESEARCH	7.50	0.00 S	
	TERM GPA : 3.000 TERM TOTALS :	10.50	6.05	26.000

WE MAKE LIVES BETTER
UT HEALTH SCIENCE CENTER
SAN ANTONIO

September 4, 2012

Mr. Saurav Pathria
8525 Floyd Curl Drive
Apt. 504
San Antonio, TX 78240

Dear Saurav

I am sorry to inform you that the Committee on Graduate Studies (COGS) of the Biochemistry program has unanimously recommended that you be dismissed from the doctoral graduate program. The COGS based their decision upon your poor academic performance, failure to remediate an "Unsatisfactory" grade in Research, and your inability to submit and defend the required Dissertation Proposal as mandated by your Supervising Committee by the end of the spring 2012 semester. It was also noted that you were absent from the lab for most of the spring semester and that you have not communicated with your department or your mentor, despite their numerous attempts to do so. I too have sent you certified mail, requesting that you contact my office by Aug. 24, 2012, to arrange a meeting to discuss your situation, but you did not respond.

Upon reviewing your history, I concur with the Biochemistry COGS' recommendation for dismissal.

Therefore, by a copy of this letter, I am asking the Registrar to terminate your enrollment as a doctoral student in the Graduate School of Biomedical Sciences effective immediately. You will need to obtain a Student Clearance Form from the Registrar's Office to officially terminate your Graduate Student status.

If you have any questions about this matter, please contact me.

Regretfully,

David S. Weiss, Ph.D.
Dean

DSW/jms

cc: Dr. Neal Robinson, COGS Chair, Biochemistry Program
    Dr. Philip Serwer, Supervising Professor, Biochemistry Program
    Dr. Bruce Nicholson, Chair, Department of Biochemistry
    Registrar's Office

GRADUATE SCHOOL OF BIOMEDICAL SCIENCES

UT HEALTH SCIENCE CENTER®

SAN ANTONIO

NOTIFICATION OF ADMISSION TO CANDIDACY

TO: __Saurav Pathria__
      Name of Student

I am pleased to inform you that the petition for your admission to candidacy for the degree of:

[   ] Master of Science

[X] Doctor of Philosophy

in the field of:

__Biochemistry__
Graduate Program

_____
IMGP Track (if applicable)

has been approved, effective this date.

_____
Dean

_____
Date   1/27/11

Distribution:
    Student (original)
    Registrar
    Chair of COGS
    Graduate Advisor
    Graduate School Office

GSBS Form 35
(07/10)

UT Health Science Center
7703 Floyd Curl Drive
San Antonio, TX 78229

Pay Group:	SAL-Salary Monthly Regular eo(s)
Pay Begin Date:	09/01/2012
Pay End Date:	09/30/2012

Business Unit: HSCSA	
Advice #:	823317
Advice Date:	10/01/2012

Saurav Pathria			
Apt # 504	Employee ID: 422831		
8525 Floyd Curl Dr	Department:	G1200-Biochemistry	
San Antonio, TX 78240-0000	Location:	Medical Sch Bld	
	Job Title:	Graduate Research Assistant	

TAX DATA:	Federal	TX State
Marital Status:	Single	n/a
Allowances:	1	0
Addl. Pct.:		
Addl. Amt.:		

HOURS AND EARNINGS

Description	Rate	Current Hours	Earnings	YTD Hours	YTD Earnings
Regular Pay		108.33	792.00	19,608.36	
Total:		108.33	792.00	19,608.36	

TAXES

Description	Current	YTD
Fed Withholding	0.00	1,929.42
Fed MED/EE	1.57	95.82
Fed OASDI/EE	4.55	277.55
Total:	6.12	2,302.79

BEFORE-TAX DEDUCTIONS

Description	Current	YTD
Total:	0.00	0.00

AFTER-TAX DEDUCTIONS

Description	Current	YTD
Total:	0.00	0.00

EMPLOYER PAID BENEFITS

Description	Current	YTD

* Taxable

	TOTAL GROSS	FED TAXABLE GROSS	TOTAL TAXES	TOTAL DEDUCTIONS	NET PAY
Current:	108.33	108.33	6.12	0.00	102.21
YTD:	19,608.36	19,608.36	2,302.79	0.00	17,305.57

Vacation Balance		Sick Balance		Personal Leave Balance	
Start Balance:	0.0	Start Balance:	0.0	Start Balance:	0.0
+ Earned:		+ Earned:		+ Earned:	
- Taken:		- Taken:		- Taken:	
+ Adjustments:		+ Adjustments:		+ Adjustments:	
End Balance:	0.0	End Balance:	0.0	End Balance:	0.0

NET PAY DISTRIBUTION

Advice #	823317	102.21
Total:		102.21

Leave Balances As of:

MESSAGE:

UT Health Science Center
7703 Floyd Curl Drive
San Antonio, TX 78229

Date
10/01/2012

Advice No.
823317

Deposit Amount: $102.21

To The
Account(s) Of

SAURAV PATHRIA
Apt # 504
8525 Floyd Curl Dr
San Antonio, TX 78240-0000

DIRECT DEPOSIT DISTRIBUTION

Account Type	Account Number	Deposit Amount
Checking	XXXXXXXXXXXXXXX	102.21
Total:		102.21

NON-NEGOTIABLE

Date-10/29/2013

Dear Dr. Weiss,

I was a PhD student in the Department of Biochemistry at UTHSCSA. I had some issues with my committee, regarding which I contacted you in February, 2012.

Due to the issues that I was facing, I offered my resignation from the program in February 2012. Somehow, University did not accept my resignation but rather dismissed me from the program in September, 2012.

The Family Educational Rights and Privacy Act (FERPA) (20 U.S.C. § 1232g; 34 CFR Part 99) is a Federal law and according to this law 'Parents or eligible students have the right to request that a school correct records which they believe to be inaccurate or misleading.

The information is misleading because my transcripts should have shown that I resigned from the program and not that I was dismissed. I am planning to go back to graduate school in some other University and this information will have an impact on my ability to get admitted in a good school.

I would highly appreciate if you could get this fixed. I could not find any other appropriate officer in the University whom I could have contacted regarding this. Since, you are the Dean of the GSBS and I believe you are already familiar with my case, I have contacted you.

Please let me know if you need any further information.

I look forward to hear from you.

Warm Regards,

Saurav Pathria

8525 Floyd Curl Dr

Apt#504, San Antonio, TX, 78240

Phone Number: (614)-264-6702

E-mail: saurav_pathria@yahoo.com

National Centre for Human Genome Studies and Research
Pharmaceutical Extension Block, Panjab University, Chandigarh – 160014.

Phones : 0172-2534109 (Office)
0172-2534118 (Direct)
E.mail: tmukhopa@hotmail.com
tmukhopa @pu.ac.in

Prof. Tapas Mukhopadhyay

Director

January 8, 2007

To Whom It May Concern

Indeed it is a great pleasure to write a letter of recommendation for Mr. Saurav Pathria. He successfully passed the National level Entrance Test of Panjab University to get enrolled in our M. Sc course in 2004 and secured First Class in final Examination held in 2006.

During his M. Sc. curriculum he got trained in many basic molecular biology techniques which he would be able to perform by himself like, Isolation of plasmids, isolation of genomic DNA and RNA, agarose gel electrophoresis PAGE, simple Chromatography, western blots, PCR, SSCP etc. He also knows other techniques like chromosome preparation, tissue processing, sectioning and other cytological and histological techniques. He had six months research training in Postgraduate Institute of Medical Education and Research, Chandigarh, and acquainted with various sophisticated instruments and their usage like FACS, phosphorimager spectrophotometer etc. Apart from that he has some expertise in Bioinformatics like how to use PubMed and NCBI data base search, primer design, alignment etc. He visited a number of Institutes in the country like NIPER, PGI, IMTECH and gathered significant amount of research interest.

Saurav appears to me as a studious and dedicated student with full of energy and enthusiasm. He is self motivated and hardworking individual who tries to develop experiments to test his hypothesis. He is very helpful and a pleasant individual who gets along well with others around him. It seems he could work in a professional environment and could adjust himself very well. He would undoubtedly be an asset to any laboratory requiring high quality research in molecular biology in general. Based on above qualities, I recommend him highly and without any reservation for the Fellowship, he is applying for future continuation of his higher studies. Please feel free to contact me should you require more information about Saurav. I wish him all success.

Tapas Mukhopadhyay, Ph.D.
Professor and Director

सूक्ष्मजीव प्रौद्योगिकी संस्थान
सेक्टर 39-ए, चण्डीगढ़, 160 036 (भारत)

INSTITUTE OF MICROBIAL TECHNOLOGY
(A CONSTITUENT ESTABLISHMENT OF CSIR)
Sector 39-A, Chandigarh-160 036 (INDIA)

इमटेक
IMTECH

To Whom It May Concern:

This is a letter of reference for Saurav Pathria, in favor of his candidacy for being considered for admission to doctoral research.

Saurav has been working in my laboratory as a Project Assistant for the last 7 months or so, after completing his Master's degree in Human Genome Studies from Panjab University. So far, he has panned a phage display library of human ScFv antibodies against two proteins (recombinant TNF-alpha, and GFP) and isolated panels of monoclonals and tested them using ELISA. In the next few months, he will participate in cloning the VH and VL regions out separately and assembling them into appropriate frameworks through splicing by overlap extension PCR to generate heavy and light chain constructs that will then be assembled together into anti-TNF-alpha antibodies. Separately, he also participates in lab discussions in our projects in enzyme engineering, protein folding and aggregation.

Saurav's understanding of the basics of molecular biology and biochemistry is excellent, and I think that his training at the Master's level has also been very good. Furthermore, phage display library screening of antibody libraries requires the grasping of a reasonably complicated set of concepts and I have had the occasion to satisfy myself over several lab seminars dealing with data interpretations that he has grasped everything that I have taught him.

Saurav's personality is pleasing, as is his temperament and his ability to get along with other members of the laboratory. His analytical skills are extremely good, and he has the correct attitude towards situations in which he finds that alternative interpretations apply; he switches his viewpoint to an alternative interpretation after satisfying himself fully that the other view is correct.

I heartily recommend Saurav's candidacy, therefore, and without any reservations. In my judgement, he has the right attitude and aptitude to do well in science, and I hope that he will find a suitable position with full financial assistance.

(Purnananda Guptasarma)   Dated : 23rd January, 2007

Dr. P. Guptasarma
Scientist, Protein Science & Engineering
Institute of Microbial Technology
Sector 39-A, Chandigarh 160 036, India
Tel : +91-172-2636680 Extn. 3301
Fax : +91-172-2690585
Email : pg@imtech.res.in

PANJAB UNIVERSITY
CHANDIGARH - 160014 (INDIA)

RAJENDRA P. DIKSHIT, Ph.D.
PROFESSOR
DEPARTMENT OF MICROBIOLOGY
BASIC MEDICAL SCIENCES BUILDING

Ref. ....
Dated *17th March 2006*

I have great pleasure in bearing the testimony to ability to Mr. Saurav Pathria, a fourth semester student of M.Sc. Human Genomics at National centre for Human Genome Studies and Research, Panjab University Chandigarh. I know Mr. Saurav for the last two years whom I have taught Molecular genetics. He is an intelligent young man who completed his bachelor's degree obtaining first class and now doing very well in M.Sc. Human Genomics. Apart from his theory courses he has done his summer training for two months at All India Institute of Medical Sciences (AIIMS) and worked on a project related to skin disease. He has also qualified GATE 2006 conducted by MHRD Govt. of India and Pre stage of other scholarship test of UGC-NET conducted by CSIR. I have found Mr. Saurav Pathria as very hardworking student and very cooperative who could work in a very friendly manner in any laboratory. In my view he will prove to be a very good research scientist in the field related to molecular biology as he has a very good exposure in this area during his M.Sc. in this university. I wish him all the best in his pursuit for academics.

Report Results

Report

Unofficial Transcript

Saurav Pathria

go to ...

| Search | Enroll | My Academics |

My Course History

Sort results by

Then by

sort

🍁 Taken   🔄 Transferred   🔷 In Progress

Course	Description	Term	Grade	Units	Status
BIOC 0003	SCIENTIFIC WRITING	Fall 2009	S	1.00	🍁
BIOC 0003	SCIENTIFIC WRITING	Fall 2010	S	1.00	🍁
BIOC 0003	SCIENTIFIC WRITING	Fall 2011	I	1.00	🍁
BIOC 5081	BIOCHEMICAL TECH LAB	Spring 2008	B	1.00	🍁
BIOC 5081	BIOCHEMICAL TECH LAB	Summer 2008	A	1.00	🍁
BIOC 5083	HYDRODYNAMIC METHODS	Spring 2008	B	2.00	🍁
BIOC 5085	BIOPHYSICAL METHODS	Spring 2008	C	2.00	🍁
BIOC 5085	BIOPHYSICAL METHODS	Spring 2010	B	2.00	🍁
BIOC 5087	MOLECULAR BIOCHEMISTRY	Spring 2009	B	2.00	🍁
BIOC 5091	SPECIAL TOPICS (Quantitative Biochemistry)	Spring 2008	B	1.00	🍁
BIOC 6010	GENE EXPRESSION	Spring 2008	B	2.00	🍁
BIOC 6035	BIOC OF MULTIMOLECULAR COMPLEX	Fall 2008	B	2.00	🍁
BIOC 6069	BIOC STUDENT REVIEW	Spring 2010	IP	1.00	🍁
BIOC 6069	BIOC STUDENT REVIEW	Fall 2010	IP	1.00	🍁
BIOC 6069	BIOC STUDENT REVIEW	Spring 2011	IP	1.00	🍁
BIOC 6069	BIOC STUDENT REVIEW	Fall 2011	S	1.00	🍁
BIOC 6071	SUPERVISED TEACHING	Fall 2009	S	1.00	🍁
BIOC 6097	RESEARCH	Summer 2008	S	5.00	🍁
BIOC 6097	RESEARCH	Fall 2008	S	1.00	🍁
BIOC 6097	RESEARCH	Spring 2009	S	5.00	🍁
BIOC 6097	RESEARCH	Summer 2009	S	6.00	🍁
BIOC 6097	RESEARCH	Fall 2009	S	5.00	🍁
BIOC 6097	RESEARCH	Spring 2010	S	6.00	🍁
BIOC 6097	RESEARCH	Summer 2010	S	6.00	🍁
BIOC 6097	RESEARCH	Fall 2010	S	7.00	🍁
BIOC 6097	RESEARCH	Spring 2011	S	8.00	🍁
BIOC 6097	RESEARCH	Summer 2011	S	6.00	🍁
BIOC 6097	RESEARCH	Fall 2011	I	7.00	🍁
BIOC 6097	RESEARCH	Spring 2012		9.00	🔷
INTD 5090	FUNDS. OF BIOMEDICAL SCIENCES I	Fall 2008	B	8.00	🍁
INTD 8002	ETHICS IN RESEARCH	Spring 2008	S	0.50	🍁
INTD 6033	CELL SIGNALING MECHANISMS	Spring 2009	A	2.00	🍁

Search Enroll My Academics

go to ...

Subject: BIOC5077

From: Venk (venkatachal@uthscsa.edu)

To: ChenH5@uthscsa.edu; Chiao@uthscsa.edu; GargN@uthscsa.edu; LiM5@uthscsa.edu; saurav_pathria@yahoo.com; UllevigS@uthscsa.edu; VillarrealMM@uthscsa.edu; pjhart@biochem.uthscsa.edu; henn@biochem.uthscsa.edu; Shiio@uthscsa.edu; sousa@biochem.uthscsa.edu; WEINTRAUB@uthscsa.edu;

Date: Thursday, April 24, 2008 2:40 PM

Dear Students and Faculty;

The first presentation in the BIOC5077 course by Saurav Pathria went off very well on April 22 with a lively discussion led by Rui Sousa and Saurav.

I am looking forward to more of the same enthusiasm for the remaining presentations. The final schedule follows.

FINAL SCHEDULE BIOC5077
Room 421B. Tuesdays or thursdays (see below) at 5.30 PM

Ying Chiao Tuesday April 29
Moderator: Lee McAlister-Henn

Cell-Permeating -Ketoglutarate Derivatives Alleviate Pseudohypoxia
in Succinate Dehydrogenase-Deficient Cells
Elaine D. MacKenzie, Mary A. Selak, Daniel A. Tennant, Lloyd J. Payne, Stuart Crosby, Casper M. Frederiksen, David G. Watson, and Eyal Gottlieb
Molecular and Cellular Biology, 27: 3282–3289, 2007

Hongzhi Chen Tuesday, May 13
Moderator; Yuzuru Shiio

Oncogenic BRAF Induces Senescence and Apoptosis through Pathways
Mediated by the Secreted Protein IGFBP7
Narendra Wajapeyee, Ryan W. Serra, Xiaochun Zhu, Meera Mahalingam, and Michael R. Green
Cell 132, 363–374, February 8, 2008

Sarah Ullevig Thursday, May 15
Moderator: Susan Weintraub

A novel anti-atherogenic role for COX-2—potential mechanism
for the cardiovascular side effects of COX-2 inhibitors
Ajay Narasimha , Junji Watanabe , James A. Lin,
Susan Hamab, Robert Langenbach, Mohamad Navab,
Alan M. Fogelman, Srinivasa T. Reddy
Prostaglandins & other Lipid Mediators 84 (2007) 24–33

Neha Garg Tuesday May 20
Moderator: Susan Weintraub

Tea Polyphenol (-)-Epigallocatechin 3-Gallate Suppresses Heregulin-â1-Induced
Fatty Acid Synthase Expression in Human Breast Cancer Cells by Inhibiting Phosphatidylinositol 3-Kinase/Akt and Mitogen-Activated Protein Kinase Cascade Signaling
Min-Hsiung Pan, Cheng-Chan Lin, Jen-Kun Lin, and
Wei-Jen Chen
J. Agric. Food Chem. 2007, 55, 5030-5037

Maria Villarreal May 27
Moderator: Lee McAlister-Henn

Nutrient-Sensitive Mitochondrial NAD+ Levels Dictate Cell Survival
Hongying Yang, Tianle Yang, Joseph A. Baur, Evelyn Perez, Takashi Matsui, Juan J. Carmona, Dudley W. Lamming, Nadja

C. Souza-Pinto, Vilhelm A. Bohr, Anthony Rosenzweig, Rafael de Cabo,
Anthony A. Sauve, and David A. Sinclair
Cell 130, 1095–1107, 2007

Mengyao Li   Thursday May 29
Moderator: Manjeri Venkatachalam

Pyruvate kinase M2 is a phosphotyrosinebinding protein
Heather R. Christofk, Matthew G. Vander Heiden, Ning Wu, John M. Asara & Lewis C. Cantley
Nature Vol 452:181-186, 2008

TheM2splice isoform of pyruvate kinase is important for cancer metabolism and tumour growth
Heather R. Christofk, Matthew G. Vander Heiden, Marian H. Harris, Arvind Ramanathan, Robert E. Gerszten, Ru Wei, Mark D.
Fleming, Stuart L. Schreiber & Lewis C. Cantley
Nature Vol 452:230-233, 2008
THESE TWO ARTICLES ARE RELATED AND WILL BE PRESENTED TOGETHER

Venk

Molecular and Cellular Biology, 27: 3282–3289, 2007

Hongzhi Chen Tuesday, May 13
Moderator: Yuzuru Shiio

Oncogenic BRAF Induces Senescence and Apoptosis through Pathways
Mediated by the Secreted Protein IGFBP7
Narendra Wajapeyee, Ryan W. Serra, Xiaochun Zhu, Meera Mahalingam, and Michael R. Green
Cell 132, 363–374, February 8, 2008

Sarah Ullevig Thursday, May 15
Moderator: Susan Weintraub

A novel anti-atherogenic role for COX-2—potential mechanism
for the cardiovascular side effects of COX-2 inhibitors
Ajay Narasimha , Junji Watanabe , James A. Lin,
Susan Hamab, Robert Langenbach, Mohamad Navab,
Alan M. Fogelman, Srinivasa T. Reddy
Prostaglandins & other Lipid Mediators 84 (2007) 24–33

Neha Garg Tuesday May 20
Moderator: Susan Weintraub

Tea Polyphenol (-)-Epigallocatechin 3-Gallate Suppresses Heregulin-â1-Induced
Fatty Acid Synthase Expression in Human Breast Cancer Cells by Inhibiting Phosphatidylinositol 3-Kinase/Akt and
Mitogen-Activated Protein Kinase Cascade Signaling
Min-Hsiung Pan, Cheng-Chan Lin, Jen-Kun Lin, and
Wei-Jen Chen
J. Agric. Food Chem. 2007, 55, 5030-5037

Maria Villarreal May 27
Moderator: Lee McAlister-Henn

Nutrient-Sensitive Mitochondrial NAD+ Levels Dictate Cell Survival
Hongying Yang, Tianle Yang, Joseph A. Baur, Evelyn Perez, Takashi Matsui, Juan J. Carmona, Dudley W.
Lamming, Nadja C. Souza-Pinto, Vilhelm A. Bohr, Anthony Rosenzweig, Rafael de Cabo,
Anthony A. Sauve, and David A. Sinclair
Cell 130, 1095–1107, 2007

Mengyao Li Thursday May 29
Moderator: Manjeri Venkatachalam

Pyruvate kinase M2 is a phosphotyrosinebinding protein
Heather R. Christofk, Matthew G. Vander Heiden, Ning Wu, John M. Asara & Lewis C. Cantley
Nature Vol 452:181-186, 2008

TheM2splice isoform of pyruvate kinase is important for cancer metabolism and tumour growth
Heather R. Christofk, Matthew G. Vander Heiden, Marian H. Harris, Arvind Ramanathan, Robert E. Gerszten, Ru
Wei, Mark D. Fleming, Stuart L. Schreiber & Lewis C. Cantley
Nature Vol 452:230-233. 2008
THESE TWO ARTICLES ARE RELATED AND WILL BE PRESENTED TOGETHER

Venk

Report Results

Return

Unofficial Transcript
Name   : Gaurav Pathria
Student ID: 5402431
Birthdate : 1981-03-26
Univ of Texas Health Science Center at San Antonio
7703 Floyd Curl Drive
San Antonio, TX 78229-3900
United States
Print Date : 2012-03-01

```
             - - - - - Academic Program History  - - - - -
Program    : Doctor of Philosophy
2007-09-13 : Admitted
             2007-09-13 : PhD in Biochemistry Major
2007-10-30 : Active in Program
```

```
          - - - - - Beginning of Graduate School Graduate Record  - - - - -
                              Sp 2008
BIOC   5081    BIOCHEMICAL TECH LAB                  3.00    3.00 B     9.000
BIOC   5083    HYDRODYNAMIC METHODS                  2.00    2.00 B     6.000
BIOC   5085    BIOPHYSICAL METHODS                   2.00    0.00 C
    Repeated   : Grade Excluded from GPA
BIOC   5091    SPECIAL TOPICS                        1.00    1.00 B     3.000
    Course Topic(s): Quantitative Biochemistry
                     Quantitative Biochemistry
BIOC   6010    GENE EXPRESSION                       2.00    2.00 B     6.000
INTD   6800    ETHICS IN RESEARCH                    0.50    0.50 S
               TERM GPA :   3.000    TERM TOTALS :  10.50    8.50    24.000

               CUM  GPA :   3.000    CUM  TOTALS :  10.50    8.50    24.000
                            Probation

                              Su 2008
BIOC   5081    BIOCHEMICAL TECH LAB                  1.00    1.00 A     4.000
BIOC   6097    RESEARCH                              5.00    5.00 S
               TERM GPA :   4.000    TERM TOTALS :   6.00    6.00     4.000

               CUM  GPA :   3.111    CUM  TOTALS :  16.50   14.50    28.000
                            Probation

                              Fa 2008
BIOC   6097    RESEARCH                              1.00    1.00 S
INTD   5000    FUNDS OF BIOMEDICAL SCIENCES I        4.00    8.00 B    24.000
               TERM GPA :   3.000    TERM TOTALS :   9.00    9.00    24.000

               CUM  GPA :   3.059    CUM  TOTALS :  25.50   23.50    52.000
                            Probation

                              Sp 2009
BIOC   5087    MOLECULAR BIOCHEMISTRY                2.00    2.00 B     6.000
BIOC   6097    RESEARCH                              5.00    5.00 S
INTD   6033    CELL SIGNALING MECHANISMS            3.00    2.00 A     8.000
               TERM GPA :   3.500    TERM TOTALS :   9.00    9.00    14.000

               CUM  GPA :   3.143    CUM  TOTALS :  34.50   32.50    66.000

                              Su 2009
BIOC   6097    RESEARCH                              6.00    6.00 S
               TERM GPA :   0.000    TERM TOTALS :   6.00    6.00     0.000

               CUM  GPA :   3.143    CUM  TOTALS :  40.50   38.50    66.000

                              Fa 2009
BIOC   0003    SCIENTIFIC WRITING                    1.00    1.00 S
BIOC   6035    BIOC OF MULTIMOLECULAR COMPLEX        2.00    2.00 B     6.000
BIOC   6271    SUPERVISED TEACHING                   1.00    1.00 S
BIOC   6097    RESEARCH                              5.00    5.00 S
               TERM GPA :   3.000    TERM TOTALS :   9.00    9.00     6.000

               CUM  GPA :   3.130    CUM  TOTALS :  49.50   47.50    72.000

                              Sp 2010
BIOC   5085    BIOPHYSICAL METHODS                   2.00    2.00 B     6.000
BIOC   6069    BIOC STUDENT REVIEW                   1.00    0.00 IP
BIOC   6097    RESEARCH                              6.00    6.00 S
               TERM GPA :   3.000    TERM TOTALS :   9.00    8.00     6.000

               CUM  GPA :   3.120    CUM  TOTALS :  58.50   55.50    78.000

                              Su 2010
```

BIOC	6097	RESEARCH		6.00	6.00 N	
		TERM GPA : 0.000	TERM TOTALS :	6.00	6.00	0.000
		CUM GPA : 3.125	CUM TOTALS :	64.50	61.50	78.000

Fa 2010

BIOC	0003	SCIENTIFIC WRITING		1.00	1.00 S	
BIOC	6069	BIOC STUDENT REVIEW		1.00	0.00 IP	
BIOC	6097	RESEARCH		7.00	7.00 S	
		TERM GPA : 0.000	TERM TOTALS :	9.00	8.00	0.000
		CUM GPA : 3.125	CUM TOTALS :	73.50	69.50	78.000

Sp 2011

BIOC	6069	BIOC STUDENT REVIEW		1.00	0.00 IP	
BIOC	6097	RESEARCH		8.00	8.00 S	
		TERM GPA : 0.000	TERM TOTALS :	9.00	8.00	0.000
		CUM GPA : 3.125	CUM TOTALS :	82.50	77.50	78.000

Su 2011

BIOC	6097	RESEARCH		6.00	6.00 S	
		TERM GPA : 0.000	TERM TOTALS :	6.00	6.00	0.000
		CUM GPA : 3.125	CUM TOTALS :	88.50	83.50	78.000

Fa 2011

BIOC	0003	SCIENTIFIC WRITING		1.00	0.00 T	
BIOC	6069	BIOC STUDENT REVIEW		1.00	1.00 S	
BIOC	6097	RESEARCH		7.00	0.00 I	
		TERM GPA : 0.000	TERM TOTALS :	9.00	1.00	0.000
		CUM GPA : 3.125	CUM TOTALS :	97.50	84.50	78.000

Sp 2012

BIOC	6097	RESEARCH		9.00		
		TERM GPA : 0.000	TERM TOTALS :	9.00	0.00	0.000
		CUM GPA : 3.125	CUM TOTALS :	97.50	84.50	78.000

Return

Subject: BIOC5077 Tuesday April 12, 5.30 PM

From: Venk (venkatachal@uthscsa.edu)

To: ChenH5@uthscsa.edu; Chiao@uthscsa.edu; GargN@uthscsa.edu; LiM5@uthscsa.edu; saurav_pathria@yahoo.com; UllevigS@uthscsa.edu; VillarrealMM@uthscsa.edu; pjhart@biochem.uthscsa.edu; henn@biochem.uthscsa.edu; Shiio@uthscsa.edu; sousa@biochem.uthscsa.edu; WEINTRAUB@uthscsa.edu;

Date: Monday, April 21, 2008 11:53 AM

Dear Students and Faculty:

We begin the BIOC5077 course tomorrow, Tuesday April 12 at 5.30 PM. The venue will be conference Room 421D.

Tomorrow's presentation will be made by Saurav Pathria. He will present the paper by De Los Rios et al. referenced below. The other paper, by Goloubinoff and deLos rios is a review in TIBS providing background material and review of the area.

The faculty member monitoring this presentation will be Rui Sousa.

I have arranged for Room 421D to be kept open. If there is any confusion, we can get the police to open the room.

Saurav, please coordinate with Biochemistry Office to make sure that the projection equipment you need is available. They expect that Esther will be in the office after 5 PM, but it is prudent to make sure that you get the projector before the office is locked.

Rui, as was the case last year, you have the option to bring snacks/pizza/whatever for the students and the handful of other attendees. Last year, we had only the students, the monitoring faculty and me in attendance.

I hope to send a final schedule soon for the remaining presentations.

I apologize for the short notice on this one.

Venk

For presentation:

Hsp70 chaperones accelerate protein translocation and the unfolding of stable protein aggregates by entropic pulling. Paolo De Los Rios, Anat Ben-Zvi, Olga Slutsky, Abdussalam Azem, and Pierre Goloubinoff 6166–6171 PNAS April 18, 2006 vol. 103 no. 16

For background:

The mechanism of Hsp70 chaperones: (entropic) pulling the models together Pierre Goloubinoff and Paolo De Los Rios. Trends in Biochemical Sciences. 2007, Vol.32, 372-380

Subject: Re: BIOC5077

From: saurav pathria (saurav_pathria@yahoo.com)

To: venkatachal@uthscsa.edu;

Date: Thursday, April 10, 2008 12:13 PM

Dear Dr. Venkatachalam,

I would like to present a paper from Dr. Rui Sousa's selection. The paper name is below:

PullingRev.companion to PNAS.
I would like to present the paper on 22nd April that is Tuesday. Please let me know if this is fine.

Thanks a lot,
Saurav Pathria.

Venk <venkatachal@uthscsa.edu> wrote:

> Dear students and faculty:
>
> Time to arrive at a schedule for the BIOC5077!
>
> You will find the articles selected by the course faculty in the form of pdf files at the following website:
>
> http://biochem.uthscsa.edu/bioc5077/
>
> The articles are really interesting and should give you insights into processes that may not necessarily be covered in the more specialized courses that you are going through. The names of the pdf files include the faculty who selected the article and key words identifying the article.
>
> I am also listing below the exclusion dates for the faculty. Students: please choose the article you would like to present and a desired date. We had agreed that the presentations would be on Tuesdays at 5.30 PM for a duration of 1 hour.
>
> John Hart: available until early June except for the week of May 12.
>
> Yuzuru Shiio: not available on the following dates: April 29, June 3, June 10
>
> Rui Sousa: not available on April 10, 11.
>
> Faculty: if you have discovered additional exclusion dates, please email me ASAP.
>
> Let me know if you have any questions
>
> Venk

Do You Yahoo!?
Tired of spam? Yahoo! Mail has the best spam protection around
http://mail.yahoo.com

Subject: RE: BIOC5077

From: Venkatachalam, Manjeri A (VENKATACHAL@uthscsa.edu)

To: ChenH5@uthscsa.edu; Chiao@uthscsa.edu; GargN@uthscsa.edu; LiM5@uthscsa.edu; saurav_pathria@yahoo.com;
          UllevigS@uthscsa.edu; VillarrealMM@uthscsa.edu; Weintraub@uthscsa.edu; HARTP@uthscsa.edu;
          shiio@uthscsa.edu; HENN@uthscsa.edu; SOUSA@uthscsa.edu;

Date: Thursday, April 17, 2008 10:27 PM

Dear All:

The final schedule is given below for your perusal. PLEASE CHECK THE SCHEDULE FOR ERRORS, CONFLICTS AND ANY CHANGES YOU WANT TO MAKE.

I WILL MAKE UP A MORE FORMAL SCHEDULE AND SEND LATER.

PLEASE NOTE THAT SAURAV PATHRIAQ IS STARTING OFF NEXT TUESDAY, APRIL 22. SAURAV AND RUI, PLEASE NOTE!!! ALL ELSE PLEASE NOTE ALSO!!!

PLEASE RESPOND WITH ANY MODIFICATIONS ASAP!!!!!

Venk

FINAL SCHEDULE BIOC5077

saurav pathria Tuesday, April 22
SOUSA: HSP70_protein_aggregates_DeLosRios_PNAS_2006
SOUSA: PullingRev.companion_to_PNAS_paper (Background)

Ying Chiao Tuesday April 29
HENN: Cell_permeant_alpha_KG_alleviate_pseudohypoxia_Mackenzie_Mol_cell_Biol_2007

Hongzhi Chen Tuesday, May 13
SHIIO: oncogenic_BRAF_senescence_apoptosis_Wajapayee_Cell_2007

Sarah Ullevig Thursday, May 15
WEINTRAUB: COX-2_antiatherogenic_Narasimha_Prost_other_lipid_mediators_2007

Neha Garg Tuesday May 20
WEINTRAUB: Tea_Polyphenol_effects_breast_cancer_cells_Pan_J_agr_Food_Chem_2007

Maria Villarreal May 27
HENN: NAD_levels_in_mitochondria_Sinclair_Cell

Mengyao Li Thursday May 29
Ella will present the work that is in the attached 2 papers in Nature
Venk is faculty for these papers

gargano   Search Mail   Search Web   saurav_pa..   Profile   ∨ Go   Sign Out   Home

Gargano at Amazon   Save on Books. Low Prices on Sports, Training, Outd...   www.Amazon.c...   Sponsored

Re: Transcript Issues   Monday, December 2, 2013 10:42 PM

From: "saurav pathria" <saurav_pathria@yahoo.com>

To: "MichaelGargano" <Gargano@uthscsa.edu>

Cc: "DavidWeiss" <weiss@uthscsa.edu>   saurav_pathria@yahoo.com

Thank you Dr. Gargano. I look forward to hearing from you

Regards,

Saurav Pathria

On Mon, 11/25/13, Gargano, Michael <Gargano@uthscsa.edu> wrote:

Subject: Re: Transcript Issues
To: "saurav pathria" <saurav_pathria@yahoo.com>
Cc: "Gargano, Michael" <Gargano@uthscsa.edu>, "Weiss, David" <weissd@uthscsa.edu>
Date: Monday, November 25, 2013, 4:44 PM

Dear Saurav,

I wanted to acknowledge receiving your email communication.
I will review this matter and schedule a time to meet with
you after Thanksgiving. I am traveling this week.

Sincerely,

Mike Gargano

Sent from my iPad

> On Nov 24, 2013, at 3:05 PM, "saurav pathria" <saurav_pathria@yahoo.com>
> wrote:
>
> Dear Dr. Gargano,
>
> I was a PhD student in the Department of Biochemistry
at the UTHSCSA. I offered my resignation to the University
in February 2012. My e-mail was deemed sufficient for the
purpose of resignation as suggested by e-mails from Dr.
Larry D. Barnes (Previous Associate Dean of Graduate School
of Biomedical Sciences) and Dr. Bruce J. Nicholson
(Chair of Department of Biochemistry) on March 12, 2012. Dr
Barnes wrote that he did not understand the purpose of my
writing e-mails after February 24, 2012 since I resigned
from the program and Dr. Nicholson in his e-mail to Dr.
Barnes asked him to accept my resignation forthwith.
Somehow, University did not accept my resignation for 6
months but rather dismissed me from the program on September
4, 2012 through a letter issued by Dr. David Weiss, Dean of
Graduate School of Biomedical Sciences.
>
> I was dismissed as per Dr. Weiss's letter. Few weeks
back, I was given a student clearance form when I went to
get my official transcripts at the registrar's office with
'voluntary withdrawal' option checked
>
> I have tried to clarify this situation with Dr. Weiss,
but he has instead referred me to you. I contacted Dr. Weiss
regarding this issue nearly a month back and the issue is
still unresolved. I hope that University is not giving me a
runaround by not giving me correct information regarding my
transcripts.
>
> I am planning to go back to graduate school in some
other University which requires transcripts from all
previous schools attended. I am worried that since

University did not accept my resignation but rather
dismissed me, it is showing up on my transcripts. A
dismissal is much worse than resignation. It is going to
have an impact on my ability to get admission in some other
school. Had University accepted my resignation, it would not
have shown on my transcripts negatively.
>
> To worsen the situation, University published the
information of my dismissal in my transcripts over the
internet. I am not sure how secured one's information is,
once it is published over the internet and if a correction
would reverse the damage done.
>
> I have attached few documents with this e-mail for your
reference. I can also forward you the e-mails of Dr. Barnes
and Dr. Nicholson, if required.
>
> I look forward to hear from you.
>
> Regards,
> Saurav Pathria
>
>
>
>
>
>
>
>
>> --- On Thu, 11/21/13, saurav pathria <saurav_pathria@yahoo.com>
wrote:
>>
>> From: saurav pathria <saurav_pathria@yahoo.com>
>> Subject: Re: Urgent: Transcript Issues
>> To: weissd@uthscsa.edu
>> Cc: gargano@uthscsa.edu
>> Date: Thursday, November 21, 2013, 11:42 AM
>> Dear Dr. Weiss:
>>
>> Thank you for your reply, but I am still looking
for answers
>> to my following questions.
>>
>> 1. I was dismissed on 09/04/2012 by a letter issued
by you.
>> Please see that letter as an attachment (SAURAV'S
Dismissal
>> UTHSCSA.pdf). In the letter you stated "I am asking
the
>> Registrar to terminate your enrollment as a
doctoral student
>> in the Graduate School of Biomedical Sciences
effective
>> immediately."
>>
>> 2. Few weeks back, I went to the registrar's office
to get
>> my official transcripts and I was given a form
which already
>> had the option of voluntary withdrawal checked by
the
>> registrar's office. I have also attached that form
(Form for
>> Transcripts.pdf) for your reference.
>>
>> 3. I am also going to attach a copy of my
unofficial
>> transcripts which I retrieved over the internet and
on the
>> first page it states, 'Dismissed-09/04/2012.'
>>
>> Now, this situation is very contradictory because
if I was
>> dismissed as per your 09/04/2012 letter and as per
my
>> unofficial transcripts then why was I not given a
form by
>> registrar's office with dismissed option checked
and
>> 09/04/2012 date written on it as a dismissal date?
>>
>> It would be nice if you could kindly clarify in
which regard
>> I should take my case to Dr. Michael Gargano (I am

sending a
>> copy of this e-mail to Dr. Michael Gargano).
>>
>>
>> Warm Regards,
>> Saurav Pathria
>>
>>
>> ---
>> On Thu, 11/21/13, Weiss, David <weissd@uthscsa.edu>
>> wrote:
>>
>> Subject: Re: Urgent: Transcripts
Correction
>> To: "saurav pathria" <saurav_pathria@yahoo.com>
>> Date: Thursday, November 21, 2013,
9:39 AM
>>
>>
>>
>>
>>
>> Dear Mr. Pathria:
>>
>>
>> I have received your emails
regarding a request to
>> correct your student record.
The UT Health Science
>> Center at San Antonio's Handbook
of Operating Procedures
>> (HOP) specifically addresses such
a student challenge to
>> their record, and I direct you to
HOP
>> Section 2.2.3 (http://www.uthscsa.edu/hop2000/2.2.3.pdf).
>> If you wish to proceed, you should
contact Dr. Michael
>> Gargano to begin advancing your
case through the proper
>> channel.
>>
>>
>>
>> Sincerely,
>>
>>
>>
>>
>>
>>
>>
>>
>>
>>
>> David S. Weiss, Ph.D.
>>
>>
>>
>>
>>
>> Professor of Physiology and
Neurology
>>
>> Dielmann Chair in Basic Biomedical
Investigation
>>
>>
>>
>>
>>
>>
>>
>>
>>
>>
>>
>>

>>
>>
>>
>>
>>
>>
>>
>>
>>
>>
>>
>>
>>
>> Dean, Graduate School of
>> Biomedical Sciences
>>
>>
>>
>> Vice President for Research,
UTHSCSA
>>
>>
>> University of Texas Health
>> Science Center at San Antonio
>>
>>
>>
>>
>>
>>
>>
>> 7703 Floyd Curl Drive
>>
>> San Antonio, Texas 78229-3900
>>
>>
>> 210.567.3712
>>
>>
>>
>>
>>
>>
>>
>>
>>
>>
>>
>>
>>
>> On Nov 14, 2013, at 3:25 PM,
saurav pathria <saurav_pathria@yahoo.com>
>> wrote:
>>
>>
>>
>>
>>
>>
>> Dear Dr. Weiss,
>>
>>
>> I wrote you an e-mail on
10/28/2013 and also sent
>> a certified letter to you on
10/29/2013 which was received
>> by University on 10/30/2013. This
is my second effort to
>> reach out to you
>>
>>

>>
>>
>> Your letter dated 09/04/2012
stated that I was dismissed
>> from the Biochemistry PhD program.
Also, my unofficial
>> transcripts reflect that I was
dismissed on 09/04/2012.
>> Few
>> weeks back, I went to the
registrar office to get my
>> transcripts and I was given a
form
>> to sign which had the option of
'voluntary
>> withdrawal' checked out and not
'dismissed'. I
>> am very confused because if I was
dismissed as per your
>> 09/04/2012 letter and as per my
unofficial transcripts
>> then
>> the option of dismissed should
have been checked by
>> registrar office. I know your
schedule must be very busy
>> but I would truly appreciate if
you could let me know as
>> to
>> what is going on with my
transcripts.
>>
>>
>>
>>
>> The e-mail sent to me by the
previous Associate Dean Dr
>> Larry D Barnes on March 12, 2012
stated: 'Since you
>> state in your message:
" ..please accept
>> this e-mail
>> as my resignation from the
program.", it is unclear
>> the
>> intent of your email messages
after February 24, 2012
>> since
>> you resigned from the program.'
>>
>>
>>
>> I don't understand that if
University already considered
>> my e-mail as a resignation from
the program then why did
>> University dismiss me from
the PhD program after 6
>> months? Should I consider this a
Defamation (Libel)?
>> Although, I could file another
lawsuit
>> based on these facts about my
transcripts (which were
>> not
>> raised in my previous lawsuit)
which I don't want unless
>> I get some remedy from the
University, I am hopeful
>> that this time we could get this
matter resolved among
>> ourselves without the involvement
>> of court or US Department of
Education, while
>> maintaining
>> utmost respect for each other.
>>
>>
>>
>> I am not sure if you know this but
I had passed all the
>> courses required by the
Biochemistry PhD program, passed
>> my
>> qualifier exam and I was a PhD
candidate. I have also
>> published a first author research

paper and written
>> another first author manuscript.
>>
>>
>>
>> You already know that I submitted
my Dissertation Proposal
>> to the committee but they never
approved it and there was
>> nothing that I could have done to
make them to approve it,
>> other than sending them continuous
reminders. Is it
>> possible
>> for the University to
>> provide me with some remedy either
by awarding me with
>> PhD
>> or correcting my transcripts and
save my career. Your
>> decision to dismiss me from the
program has closed all the
>> doors for me to pursue this career
further. I have already
>> applied for few PhD positions
>> in some Universities and have been
denied admission.
>>
>>
>>
>> For your reference, I am going to
attach my published
>> research article and another first
author manuscript that
>> I
>> wrote but never got a chance to
publish it, due to the
>> issues that I faced while at
UTHSCSA. I would highly
>> appreciate if you could kindly
look
>> at all my credentials one more
time and find a remedy
>> for
>> me.
>>
>>
>> As the saying goes: "The
>> beautiful journey of today can
only begin when we learn to
>> let go of yesterday. You will find
that it is necessary to
>> let things go, simply for the
reason that they are heavy.
>> So
>> let them go, let go of them. I
>> tie no weights to my ankles."
>>
>>
>>
>> Please let me know if you need any
information from me.
>>
>>
>> I keenly look forward to hear from
you.
>>
>>
>>
>> Warm Regards,
>>
>> Saurav Pathria
>>
>>
>>
>>
>>
>>
>>

>>
>>
>>
>>
>>
>>
>> --- On Mon, 10/28/13, saurav
pathria <saurav_pathria@yahoo.com>
>> wrote:
>>
>>
>>
>> > From: saurav pathria <saurav_pathria@yahoo.com>
>>
>> > Subject: Urgent- Transcripts
Correction
>>
>> > To:
>> weissd@uthscsa.edu
>>
>> > Date: Monday, October 28,
2013, 9:37 PM
>>
>> > Dear Dr. Weiss,
>>
>> >
>>
>> > I was a PhD student in the
Department of Biochemistry
>> at
>>
>> > UTHSCSA. I had some issues
with my committee
>> regarding
>> which
>>
>> > I contacted you in February,
2012.
>>
>> >
>>
>> > Due to the issues that I was
facing, I offered my
>>
>> > resignation from the program
in February 2012.
>> Somehow,
>>
>> > University did not accept my
resignation but rather
>>
>> > dismissed me from the program
in September, 2012.
>>
>> >
>>
>> >
>> > This information is
misleading because my transcripts
>> should
>>
>> > have shown that I resigned
from the program and not
>> that I
>>
>> > was dismissed. I am planning
to go back to graduate
>> school
>>
>> > in some other University and
this information will
>> have
>> an
>>
>> > impact on my ability to get
admitted in a good
>> school.
>>
>> >
>>
>> > The Family Educational Rights
and Privacy Act (FERPA)
>> (20
>>
>> > U.S.C. § 1232g; 34 CFR Part
99) is a Federal law
>> and

>>
>> > according to this law
'Parents or eligible students
>> have the
>>
>> > right to request that a
school correct records which
>> they
>>
>> > believe to be inaccurate or
misleading'.
>> >
>>
>> > I would highly appreciate if
you could get this
>> fixed.
>> I
>>
>> > could not find any other
appropriate officer in the
>>
>> > University whom I could have
contacted regarding
>> this.
>>
>> > Since, you are the Dean of
the GSBS and I believe you
>> are
>>
>> > already familiar with my
case, I have contacted you.
>>
>> >
>>
>> >
>>
>> > Please let me know if you
need any further
>> information.
>>
>> >
>>
>> > I look forward to hear from
you.
>>
>> >
>>
>> > Kind Regards,
>>
>> > Saurav Pathria
>>
>> >
>>
>>
>>
>>
>> <2011BACTERIOPHAGED046R1.pdf><13
>> Manuscript.pdf>
> <SAURAV's Dismissal UTHSCSA.pdf>
> <Transcripts Saurav uthscsa.pdf>
> <Form for Transcripts .pdf>

Dated-11/14/2013

Dear Dr. Weiss,

I wrote you an e-mail on 10/28/2013 and also sent a certified letter to you on 10/29/2013 which was received by University on 10/30/2013. This is my second effort to reach out to you.

Your letter dated 09/04/2012 stated that I was dismissed from the Biochemistry PhD program. Also, my unofficial transcripts reflect that I was dismissed on 09/04/2012. Few weeks back, I went to the registrar office to get my transcripts and I was given a form to sign which had the option of 'voluntary withdrawal' checked out and not 'dismissed'. I am very confused because if I was dismissed as per your 09/04/2012 letter and as per my unofficial transcripts then the option of dismissed should have been checked by registrar office. I know your schedule must be very busy but I would truly appreciate if you could let me know as to what is going on with my transcripts.

The e-mail sent to me by the previous Associate Dean Dr. Larry D Barnes on March 12, 2012 stated: 'Since you state in your message: "…please accept this e-mail as my resignation from the program.", it is unclear the intent of your email messages after February 24, 2012 since you resigned from the program.'

I don't understand that if University already considered my e-mail as a resignation from the program then why did University dismiss me from the PhD program after 6 months? Should I consider this a Defamation (Libel)? Although, I could file another lawsuit based on these facts about my transcripts (which were not raised in my previous lawsuit) which I don't want unless I get some remedy from the University. I am hopeful that this time we could get this matter resolved among ourselves without the involvement of court or US Department of Education, while maintaining utmost respect for each other.

I am not sure if you know this but I had passed all the courses required by the Biochemistry PhD program, passed my qualifier exam and I was a PhD candidate. I have also published a first author research paper and written another first author manuscript.

You already know that I submitted my Dissertation Proposal to the committee but they never approved it and there was nothing that I could have done to make them to approve it, other than sending them continuous reminders. Is it possible for the University to provide me with some remedy either by awarding me with PhD or correcting my transcripts and save my career. Your decision to dismiss me from the program has closed all the doors for me to pursue this career further. I have already applied for few PhD positions in some Universities and have been denied admission.

For your reference, I am going to attach my published research article and another first author manuscript that I wrote but never got a chance to publish it, due to the issues that I faced while at UTHSCSA. I would highly appreciate if you could kindly look at all my credentials one more time and find a remedy for me.

As the saying goes: "The beautiful journey of today can only begin when we learn to let go of yesterday. You will find that it is necessary to let things go; simply for the reason that they are heavy. So let them go, let go of them. I tie no weights to my ankles."

Please let me know if you need any information from me.

I keenly look forward to hear from you.

Warm Regards,

Saurav Pathria

--- On Mon, 10/28/13, saurav pathria <saurav_pathria@yahoo.com> wrote:

> From: saurav pathria <saurav_pathria@yahoo.com>
> Subject: Urgent- Transcripts Correction
> To: weissd@uthscsa.edu
> Date: Monday, October 28, 2013, 9:37 PM
> Dear Dr. Weiss,
>
> I was a PhD student in the Department of Biochemistry at
> UTHSCSA. I had some issues with my committee regarding which
> I contacted you in February, 2012.
>
> Due to the issues that I was facing, I offered my
> resignation from the program in February 2012. Somehow,
> University did not accept my resignation but rather
> dismissed me from the program in September, 2012.
>
> This information is misleading because my transcripts should
> have shown that I resigned from the program and not that I
> was dismissed. I am planning to go back to graduate school
> in some other University and this information will have an
> impact on my ability to get admitted in a good school.
>
> The Family Educational Rights and Privacy Act (FERPA) (20

> U.S.C. § 1232g; 34 CFR Part 99) is a Federal law and
> according to this law 'Parents or eligible students have the
> right to request that a school correct records which they
> believe to be inaccurate or misleading'.
>
> I would highly appreciate if you could get this fixed. I
> could not find any other appropriate officer in the
> University whom I could have contacted regarding this.
> Since, you are the Dean of the GSBS and I believe you are
> already familiar with my case, I have contacted you.
>
>
> Please let me know if you need any further information.
>
> I look forward to hear from you.
>
> Kind Regards,
> Saurav Pathria
>

Subject: FW: Cryo-EM

From: Pathria, Saurav (Pathria@uthscsa.edu)

To: saurav_pathria@yahoo.com;

Date: Wednesday, February 29, 2012 10:12 AM

Saurav Pathria
PhD Student,
Dept of Biochemsitry,
University of Texas HSC,
San Antonio, TX

From: Pathria, Saurav
Sent: Tuesday, February 28, 2012 12:35 PM
To: saurav_pathria@yahoo.com
Subject: FW: Cryo-EM

Saurav Pathria
PhD Student,
Dept of Biochemsitry,
University of Texas HSC,
San Antonio, TX

From: Serwer, Philip
Sent: Thursday, August 27, 2009 12:26 PM
To: Jakana, Joanita
Cc: Pathria, Saurav
Subject: Re: Cryo-EM

OK. A graduate student, Saurav Pathria, will be sending it.
Phil

On 8/27/09 12:22 PM, "Jakana, Joanita" <jjakana@bcm.tmc.edu> wrote:

It would be best to send the specimen the week of 21st September. At this time if the specimen
is good we will be able to collect images.
I will be out of the lab next week. For two weeks after I get back, we have scheduled two visitors
in addition to NCMI project.

I am looking forward to a continued collaboration.

Regards
Joanita

Subject: FW: Objectives

From: Pathria, Saurav (Pathria@uthscsa.edu)

To: saurav_pathria@yahoo.com;

Date: Monday, March 19, 2012 9:39 AM

Saurav Pathria
PhD Student,
Dept of Biochemsitry,
University of Texas HSC,
San Antonio, TX

From: Pathria, Saurav
Sent: Tuesday, September 08, 2009 5:25 PM
To: Serwer, Philip
Subject: RE: Objectives

I have run the gel today. I have not disappeared.

Saurav Pathria
PhD Student,
Dept of Biochemsitry,
University of Texas HSC,
San Antonio, TX

From: Serwer, Philip
Sent: Tuesday, September 08, 2009 5:02 PM
To: Pathria, Saurav
Subject: Re: Objectives

The qualifier is important and some time for it should be set aside. But, the proposal and exam involved should not prevent your research work from continuing.   You are at a point at which you can get much done with little enough time spent so that will have plenty of time for the proposal and the exam. Optimally, you will choose a research proposal that uses key techniques that you are likely to need for your own research. These include mass spec, recombineering and cryo-EM. That way, you will strengthen your future research while also having a more interesting proposal.

In the meanwhile, getting sample to Houston for cryo-EM means that you are leveraging your own work many fold. This opportunity should not be lost. Determining which proteins are missing in the non-aggregating mutant is part of the cryo-EM since they will likely want to use the non-aggregating 0305phi8-36 and will want to know which proteins are missing. Also, objective 2, below, is very important for the future and you should work on it during this period. The experiments involved are not either difficult or time-consuming.

   You should not "disappear" during this period. Work on both the exam and the research is both desirable and possible.

        Philip Serwer

On 9/7/09 3:25 PM, "Pathria, Saurav" <Pathria@uthscsa.edu> wrote:

Dear Dr. Serwer,

I know these are very important, but I also have to prepare for my qualifier at this time. I hope you know about qualifier exam. A student has to write a research proposal different from the field of his/her current research. I am working on it as it requires a lot of literature reading and finding an appropriate topic of research ofcourse. I will be a little occupied with this in coming days but I will try to get those experiments done as well.

I will show you the 200 words summary of the research proposal for the qualifier once I am finished writing a final draft.

I wish that we get some nice cryo-EM pictures as well and it would be nice to see which proteins are missing in non-aggregating, Delta 1 and Delta-2 mutants. I will keep you updated.

Regards,

Saurav Pathria
PhD Student,
Dept of Biochemsitry,
University of Texas HSC,
San Antonio, TX

From: Serwer, Philip
Sent: Sunday, September 06, 2009 4:31 PM
To: Pathria, Saurav
Subject: Objectives

Dear Saurav:
    Just a reminder about two important near-term objectives.
    (1) Very important is the determining of which protein (or proteins) is missing from both the non-aggregating mutant and the delta2 mutant.
        (a) The first objective is to determine the approximate molecular weight of the missing proteins. Then, scan the catalogue of 0305phi8-36 capsid proteins by molecular weight to get candidates.
        (b) The second objective is to obtain SDSPAGE with a higher resolution in the area of difference: smaller stacking gel and run the dye just off the gel. Also, place samples of the different phage next to each other and at about the same concentration.
        (c) Also, when you get a better 10% gel, run a 20% gel, to get a better picture of the lower molecular weight proteins.
        (d) We will eventually confirm by mass spec.

    (2) As a precursor to the finding conditions for the in vitro packaging pf 0305phi8-36 DNA, determine the stability of 0305phi8-36 infectivity to the following at several concentrations in broth at 28 °C:
        (a) ATP, concentrations: 0.0005 M (0.5 mM), 0.001 M (1 mM), 0.0022 M (2.2 mM), 0.005 M (5.0 mM).
        (b) Dextran mw 10,000, concentrations: 1%, 2%, 5%, 10%, 15%.
        (c) Spermidine, concentrations: 0.0005 M (0.5 mM), 0.001 M (1 mM), 0.0028 M (2.8 mM), 0.006 M (6.0 mM).

    These two are very important.

        Philip Serwer

Subject: FW: Exam

From: Pathria, Saurav (Pathris@uthscsa.edu)

To: saurav_pathria@yahoo.com;

Date: Monday, March 19, 2012 9:34 AM

Saurav Pathria
PhD Student,
Dept of Biochemsitry,
University of Texas HSC,
San Antonio, TX

From: Serwer, Philip
Sent: Sunday, February 21, 2010 6:03 PM
To: Pathria, Saurav
Subject: RE: Exam

OK. For now, just send the one sample (dialyzed main band) to Houston.
Philip Serwer

From: Pathria, Saurav
Sent: Friday, February 19, 2010 9:01 PM
To: Serwer, Philip
Subject: RE: Exam

Dear Dr. Serwer,

I think that Karen did not understand the whole thing. I have to make some changes in the written poposal like use a software to cite the references etc. The deadline for the submission of reviewed proposal is this Monday. So, it is not the exact exam. The exam will be about a week or so from that.

           You already know what I am proposing for the qualifier so I thought it would be redundant for you to go over the same thing over and over again. I have not send the reviewed copy to any of the committee members yet and I will send a copy to you as well once I send it to all the members.

           Regarding sending the sample to Houston, I am going to dialyze the sample on Sunday so that I could ship it on Monday (as it was a preference of Dr. Chang). Do you think that I should send the under 1 and under 2 band samples as well?

Regards,
Saurav Pathria
PhD Student,
Dept of Biochemsitry,
University of Texas HSC,
San Antonio, TX

From: Serwer, Philip
Sent: Friday, February 19, 2010 5:39 PM
To: Pathria, Saurav
Subject: Exam

Dear Saurav:
    Karen told me that your preliminary exam is next Monday. But, I have
not received your proposal. Presumably, the other committee members have
it. Please let me know the exact time and place of the exam and email the
proposal to me.
    Also, what is the status of the agarose gel fractionation of the cesium
chloride purified phages? And sending them to Houston?
            Philip Serwer

Subject: FW: Qualifier exam passed

From: Pathria, Saurav (Pathria@uthscsa.edu)

To: saurav_pathria@yahoo.com;

Date: Monday, March 19, 2012 9:33 AM

Saurav Pathria
PhD Student,
Dept of Biochemsitry,
University of Texas HSC,
San Antonio, TX

From: Neal Robinson [robinson@uthscsa.edu]
Sent: Thursday, March 18, 2010 11:23 AM
To: Pathria, Saurav
Subject: Re: Qualifier exam passed

Saurav,

That's great news. I took of a couple of days to go skiing in New Mexico. I'm back now, so bring the forms by my office when it is convenient.
Neal Robinson

Pathria, Saurav wrote:

> Dear Dr. Robinson,
>
> I have passed the qualifier exam. I wanted to tell you this news and also turn in the forms. I went to your office yesterday and today but could not find you. I am not sure if you are on a vacation. Please let me know whenever you are in.
>
> Regards,
> Saurav Pathria
> PhD Student,
> Dept of Biochemsitry,
> University of Texas HSC,
> San Antonio, TX

--
Neal C. Robinson, Ph.D.
Department of Biochemistry
Univ. Texas Health Science Center
San Antonio, TX 78229-3900
(210) 567-3754

Subject: FW: Samples
From: Pathria, Saurav (Pathria@uthscsa.edu)
To: saurav_pathria@yahoo.com;
Date: Wednesday, February 29, 2012 10:13 AM

Saurav Pathria
PhD Student,
Dept of Biochemsitry,
University of Texas HSC,
San Antonio, TX

From: Chang, Juan Tafu [jc131361@bcm.tmc.edu]
Sent: Thursday, June 17, 2010 12:18 PM
To: Pathria, Saurav
Subject: RE: Samples

I just got the box. Thanks.

From: Pathria, Saurav [Pathria@uthscsa.edu]
Sent: Wednesday, June 16, 2010 4:21 PM
To: Chang, Juan Tafu
Cc: Serwer, Philip
Subject: RE: Samples

Hi,

I just shipped the WT (Wild type) and RA (Reduced aggregation) samples. Both of these samples are purified by sucrose gradient and hopefully the tails are not contracted (as seen previously). Please let me know when you receive the shipment.

Thanks,
Saurav Pathria
PhD Student,
Dept of Biochemsitry,
University of Texas HSC,
San Antonio, TX

From: Chang, Juan Tafu [jc131361@bcm.tmc.edu]

Sent: Friday, June 11, 2010 10:44 AM
To: Pathria, Saurav
Subject: RE: Phi8-NA

I got EM time Saturday next week. You can send the sample any day, as long as it arrives before Sat.
There are no deliveries on weekends and holidays. Thanks!

From: Pathria, Saurav [Pathria@uthscsa.edu]
Sent: Tuesday, June 08, 2010 10:15 AM
To: Chang, Juan Tafu
Subject: RE: Phi8-NA

Hi,

I will send you the sample next week. Which day do you prefer?

Saurav Pathria
PhD Student,
Dept of Biochemsitry,
University of Texas HSC,
San Antonio, TX

From: Chang, Juan Tafu [jc131361@bcm.tmc.edu]
Sent: Tuesday, June 08, 2010 9:57 AM
To: Serwer, Philip
Cc: Pathria, Saurav
Subject: RE: Phi8-NA

Can this sample be kept at 4C for a little while? I will need to sign up for EM time this Friday to look at
the sample next week.

From: Serwer, Philip [SERWER@uthscsa.edu]
Sent: Monday, June 07, 2010 1:48 PM
To: Chang, Juan Tafu
Cc: Pathria, Saurav
Subject: Re: Phi8-NA

We have some undialyzed, reduced aggregating mutant that has not seen a cesium chloride gradient and
is still in the sucrose solution in which it was purified. Most tails are uncontracted. Saurav Pathria will

dialyze this phage and send it tomorrow. This mutant looks like the wild type, except at the tail tip where we saw more detail. We do not have a good prep of the wild type and will make another.

I will be at the Viruses of Microbes Conference in Paris from June 21-26 and will be in Europe from June 13-29. I watch my email as often as possible, while away.

On 6/6/10 8:11 PM, "Chang, Juan Tafu" <jc131361@bcm.tmc.edu> wrote:

I found the tube but there is not enough sample left, maybe 1ul. I looked in the database, which shows 13 grids were prepared from that tube, so that would have been ~50 ul. Please send more when you have time. Thanks!

From: Serwer, Philip [SERWER@uthscsa.edu]
Sent: Tuesday, June 01, 2010 6:17 PM
To: Chang, Juan Tafu
Subject: Re: Phi8-NA

Go ahead and use the sample. But, be sure that the sample is the one that went through a sucrose gradient, without the cesium chloride gradient.

On 5/31/10 5:23 PM, "Chang, Juan Tafu" <jc131361@bcm.tmc.edu> wrote:

We can revisit the carbon film to try to concentrate the phage on the grid. Last time, I used a lot of specimen trying to find the right conditions for this procedure without success. I can try again if you don't mind 'wasting' a lot of specimen.

From: Serwer, Philip [SERWER@uthscsa.edu]
Sent: Monday, May 31, 2010 2:39 PM
To: Chang, Juan Tafu
Subject: RE: Phi8-NA

I am writing from home and cannot access the images because I have forgotten the password, which is automatically entered from my computer at work. Every time that we try to concentrate the phage particles (by buoyant density centrifugation, for example), the tail contracts. We only have this one procedure for getting images of particles with uncontracted tails. Also, note that my images of negatively stained specimens indicated extensive aggregation. If we try to concentrate the phage particles, we may only succeed in aggregating them.

We have concentrated particles of other phages on support films by incubating particles with the support film before negative staining. Perhaps, the same thing will work for the cryo-EM of 8-36. I think that you should try this. After that, his tagging phage proteins is the next strategy. But, his-tagging has never been done with a phage that has so little genetics done.

From: Chang, Juan Tafu [jc131361@bcm.tmc.edu]
Sent: Saturday, May 29, 2010 12:04 AM
To: Serwer, Philip
Subject: RE: Phi8-NA

You are right. I looked through some of the images from this sample:

http://ncmidb.bcm.tmc.edu/db/record/395765/

For the most part, there are thin fibers at the baseplate region (probably DNA) but the inner tail tube is not obvious. I think I saw one contracted tail sheath, but I am not completely sure because there were other things nearby obscuring the putative inner tail tube. There were only a few images from these grids, so I did not look in there in the first pass. I think what happened was that it was dilute, so that it took a lot of searching around the grid to find some particles to image. Unfortunately, as a result there are not enough images to obtain a reconstruction that can verify the inside-out capsid theory.

I am interested in getting a reconstruction of this sample. Some people suggested using continuous carbon film as a substrate for attaching dilute particles in order to increase the concentration. I have tried this with the NA sample with little success. The carbon film tends to rip during blotting, but we can revisit this at some point. If you have some ideas on getting more particles per grid, I would like to test them out.

From: Serwer, Philip [SERWER@uthscsa.edu]
Sent: Friday, May 28, 2010 5:03 PM
To: Chang, Juan Tafu
Subject: Re: Phi8-NA

I have attached some negatively stained images of 8-36 preparations with predominantly uncontracted tails, although quite a few phage particles have lost DNA. These were preps observed in August and September, 2009, which should be about the time that we sent particles to you, assuming that we did. Do you have any 8-36 cryo-EMs from that period? I do not see any on the list below. I will check our records to see whether we sent you these sucrose gradient preps.

On 5/28/10 10:48 AM, "Chang, Juan Tafu" <jc131361@bcm.tmc.edu> wrote:

I looked through a few older dates that had >30 images and picked out a few images where the tail sheath is contracted. I assume the rest of the images from that day or grid are also contracted tail sheath. It is possible that the defocus is not the best for seeing the inner tail tube even when it is extended, or there is a mix of tails. I don't think there are images with uncontracted tail sheath in the ncmidb server, so I will ask Joanita when I see her in case she has images somewhere else.

2007/07/31 or 2007/08/17
http://ncmidb.bcm.tmc.edu/db/record/269209/ (1829)
http://ncmidb.bcm.tmc.edu/db/record/269205/ (1825)
http://ncmidb.bcm.tmc.edu/db/record/269197/ (1815)

2007/07/11
http://ncmidb.bcm.tmc.edu/db/record/260260/ (2013)
http://ncmidb.bcm.tmc.edu/db/record/260261/ (2014)
http://ncmidb.bcm.tmc.edu/db/record/260267/ (2020)
http://ncmidb.bcm.tmc.edu/db/record/260268/ (2021)
http://ncmidb.bcm.tmc.edu/db/record/260270/ (2023)

2007/07/17
http://ncmidb.bcm.tmc.edu/db/record/272000/ (1602)
http://ncmidb.bcm.tmc.edu/db/record/272001/ (1603)
http://ncmidb.bcm.tmc.edu/db/record/272007/ (1609)

2007/07/30
http://ncmidb.bcm.tmc.edu/db/record/269056/ (1304)
http://ncmidb.bcm.tmc.edu/db/record/269061/ (1309)
http://ncmidb.bcm.tmc.edu/db/record/269088/ (1335)
http://ncmidb.bcm.tmc.edu/db/record/269090/ (1337)
http://ncmidb.bcm.tmc.edu/db/record/269099/ (1346)

2007/08/22
http://ncmidb.bcm.tmc.edu/db/record/271732/ (5128)
http://ncmidb.bcm.tmc.edu/db/record/271733/ (5129)

2007/09/05
http://ncmidb.bcm.tmc.edu/db/record/273311/ (326)
http://ncmidb.bcm.tmc.edu/db/record/273319/ (328)
http://ncmidb.bcm.tmc.edu/db/record/273378/ (348)

2007/09/06
http://ncmidb.bcm.tmc.edu/db/record/272783/ (412)

http://ncmidb.bcm.tmc.edu/db/record/273460/ **(413)**

2007/09/07
http://ncmidb.bcm.tmc.edu/db/record/273403/ **(550)**
http://ncmidb.bcm.tmc.edu/db/record/273352/ **(529)**

2007/09/07
http://ncmidb.bcm.tmc.edu/db/record/273192/ **(420)**
http://ncmidb.bcm.tmc.edu/db/record/273197/ **(421)**

2007/09/10
http://ncmidb.bcm.tmc.edu/db/record/274886/ **(629)**
http://ncmidb.bcm.tmc.edu/db/record/274874/ **(617)**
http://ncmidb.bcm.tmc.edu/db/record/274873/ **(616)**
http://ncmidb.bcm.tmc.edu/db/record/274867/ **(610)**

2007/09/13
http://ncmidb.bcm.tmc.edu/db/record/274931/ **(673)**
http://ncmidb.bcm.tmc.edu/db/record/274929/ **(671)**

2007/12/18
http://ncmidb.bcm.tmc.edu/db/record/290584/ **(608)**
http://ncmidb.bcm.tmc.edu/db/record/290583/ **(607)**
http://ncmidb.bcm.tmc.edu/db/record/290582/ **(606)**

2008/02/11 (grid parked since 02/05)
http://ncmidb.bcm.tmc.edu/db/record/297941/ **(955)**
http://ncmidb.bcm.tmc.edu/db/record/297943/ **(957)**
http://ncmidb.bcm.tmc.edu/db/record/297939/ **(953) small head?**

2010/04/29
http://ncmidb.bcm.tmc.edu/db/record/311457/ **(94)**
http://ncmidb.bcm.tmc.edu/db/record/311455/ **(92)**

2010/05/30
http://ncmidb.bcm.tmc.edu/db/record/316388/ **(77)**
http://ncmidb.bcm.tmc.edu/db/record/316382/ **(71)**
http://ncmidb.bcm.tmc.edu/db/record/316379/ **(68)**

From: Chang, Juan Tafu
Sent: Thursday, May 27, 2010 8:27 PM
To: Serwer, Philip
Subject: RE: Phi8-NA

I am not sure what is happening myself.

I do not recall any images where the tail sheath has not been contracted. Do you remember when you sent the samples from the sucrose gradient? I am going to search the database for any images from around that date. Joanita might have recieved them, so I am going to ask her too when I see her.

From: Serwer, Philip [SERWER@uthscsa.edu]
Sent: Thursday, May 27, 2010 5:51 PM
To: Chang, Juan Tafu
Cc: Pathria, Saurav
Subject: Re: Phi8-NA

OK. I have scanned these micrographs. The tail sheath is invariably contracted from the tip and that phage particles are aggregated at the tip. However, the preparation that contracted from the middle was from the same gradient, but a higher density. I do not understand this. You have already looked at phages that had no contraction in the tail sheath and were alive. You also already have images of these. The phage with uncontracted sheath were less purified, having only been put through a sucrose gradient, no cesium chloride.

On 5/26/10 1:23 PM, "Chang, Juan Tafu" <jc131361@bcm.tmc.edu> wrote:

I forgot to mention that I looked at the sample at the lower density band:

http://ncmidb.bcm.tmc.edu/db/record/423975/

Indeed, my feeling is that this is a bit more concentrated, as I did not have to search the grid for a very long time to find particles. The particles are sticking together and the inner tail tube is extended. I did

http://us.mg4.mail.yahoo.com/neo/launch?.rand=67fo2epuvahh3   5/25/2012

not find any giant heads.

I don't know of any reliable way to get phages without the extended inner tail tube. However, I still think it would be very interesting to get a structure of the phage without the extended inner tail tube. Then we can confirm that the capsid is arranged inside-out. In addition, we can get some idea on how the vernier mechanism works from the 2 states. If you have more ideas on getting such as sample, I can look at the sample.

From: Serwer, Philip [SERWER@uthscsa.edu]
Sent: Friday, April 16, 2010 5:27 PM
To: Chang, Juan Tafu
Cc: Pathria, Saurav
Subject: Re: Phi8-NA

We have made some additional observations of the prep that was the source of the phage particles most recently sent. Saurav has found that one of the lower density cesium chloride gradient fractions has many more phage-like particles (3-5x more) than the fraction that we previously sent, by the criteria of both SDS gel and single-particle fluorescence microscopy. However, this fraction did not scatter a visible amount of light; that is the reason that we did not initially recognize that the phage-like particles were present. This observation is physically possible, if the particles were refractive indexed matched with the density gradient solution. In this case, they are expected to be invisible, in analogy with density matching used in x-ray scattering. A lowering of refractive index could occur if the DNA-containing shell expanded beyond the normal size, a phenomenon that we have observed with phage T3, with confirmation by cryo-EM [JMB 397, 361 (2010)]. Did you see any such particles in the fraction that you have already observed?

So, I think that this refractive index-matched fraction is worth observing by cryo-EM. Are you interested in looking at it? Saurav has seen this fraction by fluorescence microscopy and the particles look intact, but dimmer than the other phage, as though a quenching agent is inside the cavity of the shell.

Subject: FW: WT and RA 0305phi8-36 samples – status

From: Pathria, Saurav (Pathria@uthscsa.edu)

To: saurav_pathria@yahoo.com;

Date: Wednesday, February 29, 2012 10:15 AM

Saurav Pathria
PhD Student,
Dept of Biochemsitry,
University of Texas HSC,
San Antonio, TX

From: Pathria, Saurav
Sent: Friday, November 12, 2010 1:14 PM
To: Jakana, Joanita
Subject: RE: WT and RA 0305phi8-36 samples - status

Hi Joanita,

Are all the samples very dilute?

Saurav Pathria
PhD Student,
Dept of Biochemsitry,
University of Texas HSC,
San Antonio, TX

From: Jakana, Joanita [jjakana@bcm.edu]
Sent: Friday, November 12, 2010 12:07 PM
To: Pathria, Saurav
Subject: RE: WT and RA 0305phi8-36 samples - status

Hi Saurav,

I took a look at the samples you sent. They are very dilute, I did not see any aggregation in either
aliquots. Currently, I get about one particle/frame even at low mag(40K), it should be at least 30
particles. If you have a microscope it would be best to look at the prep in negative stain as an extra
concentration assay. When vitrified the concentration is about a tenth of what it is in negative stain.

Regards
Joanita

From: Pathria, Saurav [Pathria@uthscsa.edu]
Sent: Wednesday, October 27, 2010 1:10 PM
To: Jakana, Joanita
Subject: RE: WT and RA 0305phi8-36 samples

Dear Joanita,

I shipped the samples on Monday. Did you receive the package yet?

Thanks,
Saurav Pathria
PhD Student,
Dept of Biochemsitry,
University of Texas HSC,
San Antonio, TX

From: Jakana, Joanita [ijakana@bcm.edu]
Sent: Wednesday, October 20, 2010 12:25 PM
To: Pathria, Saurav
Cc: Serwer, Philip
Subject: RE: WT and RA 0305phi8-36 samples

Dear Saurav

You may go ahead and send the samples on Monday to arrive Tuesday. Thanks.

Regards
Joanita

From: Pathria, Saurav [Pathria@uthscsa.edu]
Sent: Wednesday, October 20, 2010 10:30 AM
To: Jakana, Joanita
Cc: Serwer, Philip
Subject: WT and RA 0305phi8-36 samples

Dear Juanita,

I am a graduate student in Dr. Philip Serwer's lab. I will be sending you the two samples. One sample is
WT (Wild type) and the second sample is RA (Reduced aggregating). I can send you the samples
tomorrow or on Monday. Please let me know whichever day you prefer.

Thanks,

Saurav Pathria
Graduate Student,
Dept of Biochemsitry,
University of Texas HSC,
San Antonio, TX

Subject: FW: Progress report

From: Pathria, Saurav (Pathria@uthscsa.edu)

To: saurav_pathria@yahoo.com;

Date: Monday, March 19, 2012 9:30 AM

Saurav Pathria
PhD Student,
Dept of Biochemsitry,
University of Texas HSC,
San Antonio, TX

From: Pathria, Saurav
Sent: Monday, December 13, 2010 11:23 PM
To: Serwer, Philip
Subject: Progress report

Dear Dr. Serwer,

Please see the attached report. I am planning to complete my dissertation proposal in early January. If I try to finish everything now then it won't be perfect. I want to give a nice proposal as I also have to give a departmental seminar. I have already started working on it and it will require tons of reading before I am ready for it. Anyways, I am required to finish with my committee meeting for this semester for now. I am planning to send this report to the committee by tomorrow. Please have a final look at it. I will be making a powerpoint presentation for the meeting and I will include all the future potentials of the study in that.

See you tomorrow.

Regards,
Saurav Pathria
PhD Student,
Dept of Biochemsitry,
University of Texas HSC,
San Antonio, TX

Subject: FW: Some changes

From: Pathria, Saurav (Pathria@uthscsa.edu)

To: saurav_pathria@yahoo.com;

Date: Monday, March 19, 2012 9:30 AM

Saurav Pathria
PhD Student,
Dept of Biochemsitry,
University of Texas HSC,
San Antonio, TX

From: Pathria, Saurav
Sent: Thursday, January 13, 2011 12:01 PM
To: sewer@uthscsa.edu
Subject: Some changes

Dear Dr. Serwer,

I have made some changes in the document. Changes are made in the title, introduction and specific aims.

Regards,
Saurav Pathria
PhD Student,
Dept of Biochemsitry,
University of Texas HSC,
San Antonio, TX

Reply   Reply All   Forward

Specific Aims

Pathria, Saurav

To: Hardies, Stephen C; Serwer, Philip; Haldenwang, William C; Weintraub, Susan E

Attachments: (2) Download all attachments

Specific Aims.doc (33 KB) [Open as Web Page];   Specific Aims.docx (20 KB) [Open as Web Page]

Tuesday, January 11, 2011 12:48 PM

Dear Committee Members,

I have attached the document in two different versions of
Microsoft word (new and old). I will appreciate your feedback.

Regards,
Saurav Pathria
PhD Student,
Dept of Biochemsitry,
University of Texas HSC,
San Antonio, TX

Subject: FW: Specific Aims

From: Pathria, Saurav (Pathria@uthscsa.edu)

To: saurav_pathria@yahoo.com;

Date: Monday, March 19, 2012 9:29 AM

Saurav Pathria
PhD Student,
Dept of Biochemsitry,
University of Texas HSC,
San Antonio, TX

From: Pathria, Saurav
Sent: Tuesday, January 18, 2011 1:08 PM
To: Haldenwang, William G; Hardies, Stephen C; Serwer, Philip; Weintraub, Susan E
Subject: Specific Aims

Dear Committee Members,

I have received feedback on specific aims from two of you and I am still waiting for rest to reply. I will appreciate if you can have a look at it as soon as possible. I will send you a complete dissertation proposal once I get a feedback from all of you. I am planning to get it done by the end of this month so that I can start working on each aim.

Regards,
Saurav Pathria
PhD Student,
Dept of Biochemsitry,
University of Texas HSC,
San Antonio, TX

Subject: FW: External Dissertation Committee member

From: Pathria, Saurav (Pathria@uthscsa.edu)

To: saurav_pathria@yahoo.com;

Date: Monday, March 19, 2012 9:29 AM

Saurav Pathria
PhD Student,
Dept of Biochemsitry,
University of Texas HSC,
San Antonio, TX

From: Neal Robinson [robinson@uthscsa.edu]
Sent: Monday, February 14, 2011 12:01 PM
To: Pathria, Saurav
Subject: Re: External Dissertation Committee member

Saurav,

You need to choose an external reviewer, but they don't participate in
the dissertation committee process until the final defense.
When you submit the final dissertation proposal that has been approved
by your committee, you will need to submit a NIH biosketch for the
external reviewer that you have selected.
Neal Robinson

On 2/14/2011 10:58 AM, Pathria, Saurav wrote:
> Dear Dr. Robinson,
>
> Are we supposed to have an external reviewer on our committee right now (at the time of submitting
dissertation proposal) or when a student is ready for his/her defense?
>
> Thanks.
>
> Saurav Pathria
> PhD Student,
> Dept of Biochemsitry,
> University of Texas HSC,
> San Antonio, TX
>

--
Neal C. Robinson
Dept of Biochemistry
The Univ Texas Health Sci Center
San Antonio, TX 78229-7760
(210) 567-3754

http://us.mg4.mail.yahoo.com/neo/launch?.rand=67fo2epuvahh3   5/25/2012

Subject: FW: Revised proposal
From: Pathria, Saurav (Pathria@uthscsa.edu)
To: saurav_pathria@yahoo.com;
Date: Monday, March 19, 2012 9:28 AM

Saurav Pathria
PhD Student,
Dept of Biochemsitry,
University of Texas HSC,
San Antonio, TX

From: Pathria, Saurav
Sent: Tuesday, February 22, 2011 3:12 PM
To: Serwer, Philip
Subject: Revised proposal

Dear Dr. Serwer,

Please see the attachment.

Regards,
Saurav Pathria
PhD Student,
Dept of Biochemsitry,
University of Texas HSC,
San Antonio, TX

Subject: FW: Hi

From: Pathria, Saurav (Pathria@uthscsa.edu)

To: saurav_pathria@yahoo.com;

Date: Monday, March 19, 2012 9:27 AM

Saurav Pathria
PhD Student,
Dept of Biochemsitry,
University of Texas HSC,
San Antonio, TX

From: Pathria, Saurav
Sent: Wednesday, March 16, 2011 2:42 PM
To: Serwer, Philip
Subject: Hi

Dear Dr Serwer,

Few things:

1. I need to find an external examiner for my dissertation. Though he/she will be involved in the final stages of the PhD, a name has to be proposed and given to the graduate school by me. Please let me know your suggestions.

2. I think it would be in our best interest if we talk to the group in Purdue about the T3 cryo-EM and ask them about their suggestions on the residues that we have planned to change. They might have some extra information which we might be lacking right now. Also, it would be worth asking them about interactions which they think are the most important.

3. The general procedure is that a student shows the proposal to his/her supervisor and then presents a seminar. I am trying to get feedback from committee members right now so that I can present what everyone agrees on. If it takes them a lot of time to get back to me then I will just present it and then get their suggestions in the meeting. I will show you a powerpoint presentation as soon as possible.

Regards,
Saurav Pathria
PhD Student,
Dept of Biochemsitry,
University of Texas HSC,
San Antonio, TX

Subject: FW: Dissertation Proposal Seminar

From: Pathria, Saurav (Pathria@uthscsa.edu)

To: saurav_pathria@yahoo.com;

Date: Monday, March 19, 2012 9:26 AM

Saurav Pathria
PhD Student,
Dept of Biochemsitry,
University of Texas HSC,
San Antonio, TX

From: Pathria, Saurav
Sent: Friday, April 08, 2011 1:08 PM
To: Serwer, Philip; Hardies, Stephen C; Haldenwang, William G; Weintraub, Susan E
Subject: Dissertation Proposal Seminar

Dear Committee Members,

Could you please let me know your availability in coming weeks. I have to give a departmental seminar of my proposal. I have made some changes in the regions of mutation in gp10A. I will send you a revised version of the proposal very soon. Usually students give a departmental presentation before the committee meeting. But, I would like to have a meeting with all of you before I proceed to give a seminar. I would like to have all of you on the same page before this seminar.

Regards,
Saurav Pathria
PhD Student,
Dept of Biochemsitry,
University of Texas HSC,
San Antonio, TX

Subject:	FW: Revised Proposal
From:	Pathria, Saurav (Pathria@uthscsa.edu)
To:	saurav_pathria@yahoo.com;
Date:	Monday, March 19, 2012 9:26 AM

Saurav Pathria
PhD Student,
Dept of Biochemsitry,
University of Texas HSC,
San Antonio, TX

From: Pathria, Saurav
Sent: Monday, April 11, 2011 4:25 PM
To: Serwer, Philip
Subject: Revised Proposal

Dear Dr. Serwer,

Please see the attached revised proposal. There are significant changes in the regions of interest, other than that everything else stays pretty much the same. I will send it to other members of the committee once you have looked at it.

Regards,
Saurav Pathria
PhD Student,
Dept of Biochemsitry,
University of Texas HSC,
San Antonio, TX

Subject: FW: Revised Proposal

From: Pathria, Saurav (Pathria@uthscsa.edu)

To: saurav_pathria@yahoo.com;

Date: Monday, March 19, 2012 9:25 AM

Saurav Pathria
PhD Student,
Dept of Biochemsitry,
University of Texas HSC,
San Antonio, TX

From: Pathria, Saurav
Sent: Sunday, April 17, 2011 11:33 PM
To: Serwer, Philip
Subject: Revised Proposal

Dear Dr. Serwer,

I have made changes. If you can have a look at it tomorrow (April 18, Monday) then I will send it to other committee members by Tuesday. I am planning to schedule a meeting on April 27 and give a departmental presentation on April 28 (these are the two days when other members are available). Will these two days fit your schedule?

Also, Dr. Wen Jiang has agreed to be on my committee as an 'external reviewer'.

Regards,
Saurav Pathria
PhD Student,
Dept of Biochemsitry,
University of Texas HSC,
San Antonio, TX

Subject:	FW: Committee meeting
From:	Pathria, Saurav (Pathria@uthscsa.edu)
To:	saurav_pathria@yahoo.com;
Date:	Monday, March 19, 2012 9:25 AM

Saurav Pathria
PhD Student,
Dept of Biochemsitry,
University of Texas HSC,
San Antonio, TX

From: Pathria, Saurav
Sent: Friday, April 22, 2011 12:52 PM
To: Serwer, Philip; Haldenwang, William G; Weintraub, Susan E; Hardies, Stephen C
Subject: Committee meeting

Dear Committee members,

I have attached a revised version of the dissertation proposal in a pdf format. I have also reserved a conference room for meeting based on your availability. Please see the schedule below:

4/28/2011
Room 421B
10am-1pm

I will schedule a departmental presentation after this meeting. Could you please let me know your schedule for the week after next (May2-6).

Regards,
Saurav Pathria
PhD Student,
Dept of Biochemsitry,
University of Texas HSC,
San Antonio, TX

Subject: FW: Dissertation Proposal and Committee meeting

From: Pathria, Saurav (Pathria@uthscsa.edu)

To: saurav_pathria@yahoo.com;

Date: Monday, March 19, 2012 9:24 AM

Saurav Pathria
PhD Student,
Dept of Biochemsitry,
University of Texas HSC,
San Antonio, TX

From: Neal Robinson [robinson@uthscsa.edu]
Sent: Thursday, April 28, 2011 11:54 AM
To: Pathria, Saurav
Subject: Re: Dissertation Proposal and Committee meeting

Saurav,

The Form 30,
available at
http://gsbs.uthscsa.edu/files/resource/w2/82/rsrc/FORM_30_-
_Dissertation_Proposal_Committee_Approval.pdf
signed by all of the committee members will replace the normal committee
meeting forms. If the committee members do not sign the form because
they did not approve of the disseration and require revisions, you
should turn in to me the normal sheets so that I can see comments.

Once the committee approves of the disseration, you need to submit to me
a pdf copy of the disseration, and an NIH biosketch of your outside member.

Neal Robinson
Chair of Biochemistry COGS

, On 4/27/2011 1:08 PM, Pathria, Saurav wrote:
> Dear Dr. Robinson,
>
> Are we required to have the grades form signed by the committee when we meet with the committee
for our dissertation proposal or we have to get the form for the approval of the proposal signed? I
believe that we don't require a separate meeting for the semester after this meeting, right?
>
> Regards,
> Saurav Pathria
> PhD Student,
> Dept of Biochemsitry,
> University of Texas HSC,

> San Antonio, TX

--
Neal C. Robinson
Dept of Biochemistry
The Univ Texas Health Sci Center
San Antonio, TX 78229-7760
(210) 567-3754

Subject: FW: Dissertation proposal
From: Pathria, Saurav (Pathria@uthscsa.edu)
To: saurav_pathria@yahoo.com;
Date: Tuesday, March 20, 2012 8:53 AM

Saurav Pathria
PhD Student,
Dept of Biochemsitry,
University of Texas HSC,
San Antonio, TX

From: Weintraub, Susan E
Sent: Thursday, May 19, 2011 5:53 PM
To: Pathria, Saurav; Hardies, Stephen C; Haldenwang, William G
Subject: RE: Dissertation proposal

Hi Saurav,

I'll send you a file with my comments tomorrow.

Regards,

Sue Weintraub

******

Susan T. Weintraub, Ph.D.
Professor, Department of Biochemistry
MC 7760
The University of Texas Health Science
  Center at San Antonio
7703 Floyd Curl Drive
San Antonio, Texas 78229-3900
(210) 567-4043
(210) 567-5524 (fax)
weintraub@uthscsa.edu

From: Pathria, Saurav
Sent: Thursday, May 19, 2011 1:35 PM
To: Hardies, Stephen C; Weintraub, Susan E; Haldenwang, William G
Subject: Dissertation proposal

Dear Committee members,

Please let me know if you did get a chance to read the revised proposal.

Thank you.

Regards,
Saurav Pathria
PhD Student,
Dept of Biochemsitry,
University of Texas HSC,
San Antonio, TX

Subject: FW: Dissertation proposal

From: Pathria, Saurav (Pathria@uthscsa.edu)

To: saurav_pathria@yahoo.com;

Date: Tuesday, March 20, 2012 8:54 AM

Saurav Pathria
PhD Student,
Dept of Biochemsitry,
University of Texas HSC,
San Antonio, TX

From: Phillip Serwer [serwer@uthscsa.edu]
Sent: Saturday, June 18, 2011 3:41 PM
To: Pathria, Saurav
Subject: Re: Dissertation proposal

Saurav:
    I have attached the comments of Drs. Weintraub (click on the yellow indicators to see notes) and Hardies
on your dissertation proposal. Please make the changes in grammar that Dr. Weintraub indicates. Also, if
you agree with suggested changes in content from either Dr. Weintraub or Dr. Hardies, make those changes
also. If you either have a question about a suggested change or disagree, don't yet make the change. We
will discuss the latter when I return. Whatever you do, do not make a major change in either the organization
or the content.
    Please also send me a copy of the draft that you produce as a result of changes made before we discuss.
I will be watching my email, but maybe not every day.
        Philip Serwer

Subject: FW: Revised Proposal

From: Pathria, Saurav (Pathria@uthscsa.edu)

To: saurav_pathria@yahoo.com;

Date: Tuesday, March 20, 2012 8:55 AM

Saurav Pathria
PhD Student,
Dept of Biochemsitry,
University of Texas HSC,
San Antonio, TX

From: Pathria, Saurav
Sent: Monday, July 04, 2011 6:33 PM
To: Weintraub, Susan E
Subject: Revised Proposal

Dear Dr. Weintraub,

I have made changes based on your suggestions. Please see the revised draft in a pdf format.

Regards,
Saurav Pathria
PhD Student,
Dept of Biochemsitry,
University of Texas HSC,
San Antonio, TX

Subject: FW: Revised Proposal

From: Pathria, Saurav (Pathria@uthscsa.edu)

To: saurav_pathria@yahoo.com;

Date: Tuesday, March 20, 2012 8:54 AM

Saurav Pathria
PhD Student,
Dept of Biochemsitry,
University of Texas HSC,
San Antonio, TX

From: Pathria, Saurav
Sent: Monday, July 04, 2011 6:30 PM
To: Hardies, Stephen C
Subject: Revised Proposal

Dear Dr. Hardies,

I have made few changes based on your recommendations. The significance part is in the background and significance section where I talk about T3. Regarding mutating residues in the two regions at the same time to check that the effect is actually due to a salt bridge and not due to shifting of the residue to interact with the next one, I have made a change there. Since, a structure for T3 to a very high resolution is lacking, I have to rely on visual observation to pick residues for mutation, which I believe should be very close. Regarding that recent JBC paper on T7 structure by a group in Spain, I am not very excited about it. First of all they have tried to make T3 look just like HK97 which I believe is not the case entirely. Secondly, their resolution is 1 nm, which is not very good either. The structure which I have from Purdue has a resolution of about 0.4 nm.

I have attached the draft in a pdf format.

Regards,
Saurav Pathria
PhD Student,
Dept of Biochemsitry,
University of Texas HSC,
San Antonio, TX

Subject: FW: Courses
From: Pathria, Saurav (Pathria@uthscsa.edu)
To: saurav_pathria@yahoo.com;
Date: Tuesday, March 20, 2012 9:26 AM

Saurav Pathria
PhD Student,
Dept of Biochemsitry,
University of Texas HSC,
San Antonio, TX

From: Pathria, Saurav
Sent: Friday, July 30, 2010 11:19 AM
To: Robinson, Neal C
Subject: RE: Courses

Thanks Dr. Robinson.

Saurav Pathria
PhD Student,
Dept of Biochemsitry,
University of Texas HSC,
San Antonio, TX

From: Neal Robinson [robinson@uthscsa.edu]
Sent: Friday, July 30, 2010 11:15 AM
To: Pathria, Saurav
Subject: Re: Courses

Saurav,

You need to enroll for 9 credits.
Since you have taken all of your advanced courses, but haven't written your proposal you should enroll in the
following courses:
1 credit of Biochemistry Student Review
1 credit of Scientific Writing
7 credits of Research

You can only enroll in Dissertation if your Dissertation Proposal has been approved by COGS and submitted to the
Graduate Dean's office.
Neal Robinson

Pathria, Saurav wrote:

Dear Dr. Robinson,

Please let me know the courses for which I need to enroll for this fall. Do I need to enroll for BIOC-

7099 DISSERTATION?

Thanks.

Regards,
Saurav Pathria
PhD Student,
Dept of Biochemsitry,
University of Texas HSC,
San Antonio, TX

--
Neal C. Robinson, Ph.D.
Department of Biochemistry
Univ. Texas Health Science Center
San Antonio, TX 78229-3900
(210) 567-3754

Subject: FW: Brief manuscript
From: Pathria, Saurav (Pathria@uthscsa.edu)
To: saurav_pathria@yahoo.com;
Date: Monday, March 26, 2012 9:55 AM

Saurav Pathria
PhD Student,
Dept of Biochemsitry,
University of Texas HSC,
San Antonio, TX

From: Serwer, Philip
Sent: Friday, May 13, 2011 6:04 PM
To: Pathria, Saurav
Cc: philipserwer@sbcglobal.net
Subject: Brief manuscript

Saurav:
While you are working on T3, we can try to get in shape a manuscript on your older work on 0305phi8-36. I
have attached a draft. Please get the table on the phage titers ready so that we can send it to Dr. Hardies next
week. Also, now is the time to comment on the draft.
Philip Serwer

Subject: FW: Draft

From: Pathria, Saurav (Pathria@uthscsa.edu)

To: saurav_pathria@yahoo.com;

Date: Monday, March 26, 2012 9:55 AM

Saurav Pathria
PhD Student,
Dept of Biochemsitry,
University of Texas HSC,
San Antonio, TX

From: Pathria, Saurav
Sent: Sunday, May 15, 2011 3:51 PM
To: Serwer, Philip
Subject: Draft

Dear Dr. Serwer,

I have attached the table. I think one of the previous drafts that you made had a lot of details about mimiviruses and other large DNA viruses. Any specific reason for which you omitted that part? I think that it was pretty impressive and it seemed more significant from evolutionary point of view. Your theme here in this draft is fine but in my opinion a bigger picture was formed when you had a comparative analysis with other viruses having large DNA.

I would emphasize more on the clustering or island formation (though propagation in a biofilm is a function associated with clustering). The point here is that 1. Why do these genes tend to cluster together? 2. Why are these genes non-essential under laboratory conditions (though they do provide some growth advantage)? 3. Is clustering or island formation a way by which new (species) and virulent viruses (by accumulation of PAI's-Pathogenicity Islands and other genes) are formed 4. Why does clustering or island formation take place between genes associated in a related function? 5. We have isolated these deletion mutants (variants) among a major population (wild type). I am not even sure if it is correct to call them deletion mutants. Since, these are actually variants. A possible reason would be that the nature is accumulating more and more genes (seen as cellular homologous gene islands in the wild type) but still keeping some variants in this major population. Why is it still carrying around these variants? Is is possible that it had very less DNA initially (even less than the two variants) and these variants represent one of the remnants during this evolutionary process. It is probably acquiring more and more cellular genes to gain advantage for the future.

Previous studies have recognized 'cellular gene homologs', but as far as I know, no one has shown that some of these homologs (except tRNAs) are of no or very little advantage to the phage under laboratory conditions. Our study has solved atleast one very important puzzle i.e., related to their function. One island is absolutely non-essential but one island provides a growth advantage.Your orginal hypothesis in Virology Journal 'Evolution and the complexity of bacteriophages' is tested in this study.

I would just say that we have isolated two variants in wild type 8-36 population. These variants are very less in number compared to the wild type population. Their less number would indicate that phage is acquiring new genes and this why they are left in very less numbers. Since, the phage (major population) is still carrying around these variants, would mean a way to avoid adverse environmental effects and then propagate as a major population in the form of a variant. A very inriguing biological phenomenon takes place when phage picks up these cellular gene homologs. This phenonmenon involes joining of functionally similar genes which we call as islands. Now, in my opinion the translocation operon was not picked up all at once but instead the genes got inserted one by one and presence of a structal gene 'moron' in between this operon proves this hypothesis. If this whole operon was inserted all at once then there won't be any other gene sitting inside. Same holds true for second island. The genes present in this island are all involved with proteins somehow from synthesis to avoiding misfolding to inserting metals in proteins etc. What does all this point to????????

In my opinion genes have the potential to recognize adjacent genes and have a sense where they should get inserted in the whole genome. It is quite possible that after several generations that 'moron' gene will be thrown out or inserted somewhere else in the genome. Said that, we have variants which don't have these two islands? What does this tell us???? Well, phage can survive without these islands but clearly it gets a growth advantage by keeping the second island. We now know that their is some advantage of keeping these islands. Though we could not find advantage of keeping the first island, it might be essential in biofilm-propagation as you proposed.

So we have shown that addition of these islands in not in vain. It definitely has some advantage for the phage. Three very important biological phenomenons are going on here:

1. Functionally related genes (cellular homologs) tend to form islands in the 8-36 genome
2. Formation of these islands takes place by insertion of one functionally related gene at a time
3. These islands provide advantage to the phage to adapt to the ever changing environment

I think we have to say these points very loudly in our paper. I won't be suprised if this could open a new window for other researchers to study as to why only the functionally related genes join together in these islands. If this phenomenon is true then this could be the reason that we see most of the essential genes together (on the left side of the genome, I think in 8-36). This could help us in answering bigger questions like what determines sequence of genes in a genome, what triggers genes to move in and out, which factor decides where exactly a gene should be inserted (is the potential to decide this present in the gene or other factors impact that?)

I don't think that there is any harm in being overambitious and giving it a shot in either nature or science journal even as a small paper (in the form of a letter).

I have also attached the draft with my comments on it.

Regards,
Saurav Pathria
PhD Student,
Dept of Biochemsitry,
University of Texas HSC,
San Antonio, TX

Subject: FW: The manuscript that goes with the table

From: Pathria, Saurav (Pathria@uthscsa.edu)

To: saurav_pathria@yahoo.com;

Date: Monday, March 26, 2012 9:56 AM

Saurav Pathria
PhD Student,
Dept of Biochemsitry,
University of Texas HSC,
San Antonio, TX

From: Phillip Serwer [serwer@uthscsa.edu]
Sent: Wednesday, June 29, 2011 2:20 PM
To: Pathria, Saurav
Subject: Re: The manuscript that goes with the table

Saurav:
   I have attached the manuscript that goes with the table that I just sent. Please provide the missing material indicated by ---, by hand writing it on a paper copy. I will enter it in the manuscript. Also, the content of Figure 3 remains to be decided and this will have to be discussed with Dr. Hardies after I forward to him the rest of the manuscript with the material now missing inserted.
      Philip Serwer

Subject: FW: Hi

From: Pathria, Saurav (Pathria@uthscsa.edu)

To: saurav_pathria@yahoo.com;

Date: Monday, March 26, 2012 9:56 AM

Saurav Pathria
PhD Student,
Dept of Biochemsitry,
University of Texas HSC,
San Antonio, TX

From: Pathria, Saurav
Sent: Monday, July 25, 2011 12:29 PM
To: Hardies, Stephen C
Subject: RE: Hi

I have asked Dr. Serwer and there is no change in the draft from its previous version. I have attached the previous version, table, and the latest image of the conserved genes. I am not sure if the table is right or it need changes.

Regards,
Saurav Pathria
PhD Student,
Dept of Biochemsitry,
University of Texas HSC,
San Antonio, TX

From: Stephen C. Hardies [hardies@uthscsa.edu]
Sent: Monday, July 25, 2011 10:44 AM
To: Pathria, Saurav
Subject: Re: Hi

Saurav:

OK; I fell behind with the other paper I was working on, so it will be later this week. E-mail me a copy of the table, and of the draft as it now stands.

Steve Hardies

> Dear Dr. Hardies,
>
> I have to complete that table which has to be sent in the 8-36 paper.
> Please let me know whenever you have time this week.
>

> Regards,
> Saurav Pathria
> PhD Student,
> Dept of Biochemsitry,
> University of Texas HSC,
> San Antonio, TX
>

Subject: FW: Dissertation Proposal
From: Pathria, Saurav (Pathria@uthscsa.edu)
To: saurav_pathria@yahoo.com;
Date: Monday, March 12, 2012 12:41 PM

Saurav Pathria
PhD Student,
Dept of Biochemsitry,
University of Texas HSC,
San Antonio, TX

From: Pathria, Saurav
Sent: Tuesday, August 02, 2011 11:10 AM
To: Hardies, Stephen C; Weintraub, Susan E
Subject: Dissertation Proposal

Dear Committee Members,

I am pretty late in submitting my dissertation proposal. I would appreciate if you could have a final look at it.

Thank you.

Regards,
Saurav Pathria
PhD Student,
Dept of Biochemsitry,
University of Texas HSC,
San Antonio, TX

Print
Page 1 ot 1

Subject: FW: Dissertation proposal
From: Pathria, Saurav (Pathria@uthscsa.edu)
To: saurav_pathria@yahoo.com;
Date: Monday, March 12, 2012 12:42 PM

Saurav Pathria
PhD Student,
Dept of Biochemsitry,
University of Texas HSC,
San Antonio, TX

From: Pathria, Saurav
Sent: Friday, August 26, 2011 1:21 PM
To: Hardies, Stephen C; Weintraub, Susan E
Subject: Dissertation proposal

Dear Members of the Committee,

I am looking forward to hear from you.

Thank you.

Saurav Pathria
PhD Student,
Dept of Biochemsitry,
University of Texas HSC,
San Antonio, TX

http://us.mg4.mail.yahoo.com/neo/launch?.rand=67fo2epuvahh3   5/25/2012

Subject: FW: Rough (very) draft of a full-length manuscript on 8-36

From: Pathria, Saurav (Pathria@uthscsa.edu)

To: saurav_pathria@yahoo.com;

Date: Monday, March 26, 2012 9:57 AM

Saurav Pathria
PhD Student,
Dept of Biochemsitry,
University of Texas HSC,
San Antonio, TX

From: Phillip Serwer [serwer@uthscsa.edu]
Sent: Tuesday, September 20, 2011 2:40 PM
To: Pathria, Saurav
Cc: Hardies, Stephen C
Subject: Rough (very) draft of a full-length manuscript on 8-36

Saurav:
I have attached the rough draft. I will generate Figures 3 and 4. You
have already given me enough have enough for Figure 5. The rest is for you
to do. Please assemble figures 1-2 and the two tables.
The references are part done. Please let me know about any others that
should be included.
Philip Serwer

Subject: FW: Figure and table

From: Pathria, Saurav (Pathria@uthscsa.edu)

To: saurav_pathria@yahoo.com;

Date: Tuesday, February 28, 2012 12:44 PM

Saurav Pathria
PhD Student,
Dept of Biochemsitry,
University of Texas HSC,
San Antonio, TX

From: Phillip Serwer [serwer@uthscsa.edu]
Sent: Wednesday, September 28, 2011 4:27 PM
To: Pathria, Saurav
Subject: Re: Figure and table

Figure 1 has a positioning problem in (b). Also, please send a jpg of this
figure.
        Philip Serwer

On 9/28/11 3:41 PM, "Pathria, Saurav" <Pathria@uthscsa.edu> wrote:

> I have attached figure 1 and table with titers.
>
> Saurav Pathria
> PhD Student,
> Dept of Biochemsitry,
> University of Texas HSC,
> San Antonio, TX
>
> From: Phillip Serwer [serwer@uthscsa.edu]
> Sent: Wednesday, September 28, 2011 1:36 PM
> To: Pathria, Saurav
> Subject: Next draft
>
> Saurav:
>   I have attached the next draft, together with figures 4 and 5. This is
> the time to review the whole manuscript very carefully, including the
> checking of all statements for accuracy and the filling of blanks.
>   Philip Serwer

RE: Dissertation Proposal

Weintraub, Susan E
Sent: Tuesday, October 18, 2011 3:28 PM
To: Pathria, Saurav; Hardies, Stephen C
Cc: Serwer, Philip; Haldenwang, William G

Hi Saurav,

I will look at your proposal by the end of the week. I have several deadlines before then.

Regards,

Sue Weintraub

******

Susan T. Weintraub, Ph.D.
Professor, Department of Biochemistry
Director, Mass Spectrometry Laboratory
The University of Texas Health Science Center
   at San Antonio
7703 Floyd Curl Drive
MC 7760
San Antonio, Texas 78229-3900
(210) 567-4043
(210) 567-5524 (fax)
weintraub@uthscsa.edu

From: Pathria, Saurav
Sent: Tuesday, October 18, 2011 3:21 PM
To: Weintraub, Susan E; Hardies, Stephen C
Cc: Serwer, Philip; Haldenwang, William G
Subject: Dissertation Proposal

Dear Committee Members,

It has been nearly 4 months since I last sent you updated dissertation proposal. Even after my repeated request, I have still not heard back from you. Some of you had comments based on which I did make changes in the last draft that I sent you. I am already very late in submitting the dissertation proposal (according to our graduate handbook). I would appreciate if without any further delay you can approve it or if you have further comments send it back to me.

I look forward to hear from you soon.

Thank you.

Regards,

Saurav Pathria
PhD Student,
Dept of Biochemsitry,
University of Texas HSC,
San Antonio, TX

Subject: FW: Manuscript

From: Pathria, Saurav (Pathria@uthscsa.edu)

To: saurav_pathria@yahoo.com:

Date: Monday, March 26, 2012 9:58 AM

Saurav Pathria
PhD Student,
Dept of Biochemsitry,
University of Texas HSC,
San Antonio, TX

From: Phillip Serwer [serwer@uthscsa.edu]
Sent: Wednesday, October 26, 2011 4:41 PM
To: Pathria, Saurav
Subject: FW: Manuscript

I have attached the manuscript that I forgot to attqch when I sent the
figures and tables.
Philip Serwer

Subject: FW: 8-36

From: Pathria, Saurav (Pathria@uthscsa.edu)

To: saurav_pathria@yahoo.com;

Date: Wednesday, February 29, 2012 10:24 AM

Saurav Pathria
PhD Student,
Dept of Biochemsitry,
University of Texas HSC,
San Antonio, TX

From: Stephen C. Hardies [hardies@uthscsa.edu]
Sent: Thursday, November 03, 2011 3:42 PM
To: Pathria, Saurav
Subject: RE: 8-36

Saurav:

I don't feel a need to review it, but if you want to send the final
version I may be able to find time to briefly look over it.

Steve

> Dear Dr. Hardies,
>
> I think the manuscript is finished now. I believe Dr. Serwer and I would
> like you to read the final draft before we submit it and have your
> comments (if any) taken care of before submission.
>
> Regards,
> Saurav Pathria
> PhD Student,
> Dept of Biochemsitry,
> University of Texas HSC,
> San Antonio, TX
>
> From: Stephen C. Hardies [hardies@uthscsa.edu]
> Sent: Wednesday, November 02, 2011 10:41 PM
> To: Pathria, Saurav
> Subject: Re: 8-36
>
> Saurav:
>
> If it's in final form, you should submit it. If it's not, finish it. If
> you really need me to work on this manuscript yet another time, you're
> going to have to wait till I clear some other jobs off my desk. I agree

> that it would be better if you could finish it yourselves and not have to
> wait for me.
>
> Steve
>
>> Dear Dr. Hardies,
>>
>>
>>
>> NCBI keeps on receiving new sequences at a particular rate. I am saying
>> this because our informatics might not mean a lot if we wait longer and
>> longer. I am pretty sure if we do informatics after a month or two we
>> might find more genes matching from some newly sequenced phage. So, it
>> might in our best interest to get this paper out as soon as possible to
>> avoid a third round of informatics. I believe this latest informatics is
>> already 3 months old. This is my opinion, but you certainly know a lot
>> more than I do about how much it might change etc.
>>
>>
>>
>> Regards,
>>
>> Saurav Pathria
>> PhD Student,
>> Dept of Biochemsitry,
>> University of Texas HSC,
>> San Antonio, TX
>>

Subject: FW: Report Fall 2011

From: Pathria, Saurav (Pathria@uthscsa.edu)

To: saurav_pathria@yahoo.com;

Date: Tuesday, March 20, 2012 8:55 AM

Saurav Pathria
PhD Student,
Dept of Biochemsitry,
University of Texas HSC,
San Antonio, TX

From: Pathria, Saurav
Sent: Tuesday, November 29, 2011 4:48 PM
To: Serwer, Philip
Subject: Report Fall 2011

Dear Dr. Serwer,

I have written the report for the scientific writing part of this semester. Please see the attached file. I have also printed out a hardcopy for you. Sometimes there are compatibility issues between a mac and windows pc. If you see something not right then please let me know. Since, I could not find you in your office, I have placed the hardcopy (I believe you prefer this) on my desk or I will bring over the hardcopy to your office tomorrow.

Thank you.

Regards,
Saurav Pathria
PhD Student,
Dept of Biochemsitry,
University of Texas HSC,
San Antonio, TX

Subject:	FW: Progress Report (Fall 2011)
From:	Pathria, Saurav (Pathria@uthscsa.edu)
To:	saurav_pathria@yahoo.com;
Date:	Sunday, March 18, 2012 8:59 PM

Saurav Pathria
PhD Student,
Dept of Biochemsitry,
University of Texas HSC,
San Antonio, TX

From: Pathria, Saurav
Sent: Thursday, December 08, 2011 4:28 PM
To: Serwer, Philip; Haldenwang, William G; Weintraub, Susan E; Hardies, Stephen C
Subject: Progress Report (Fall 2011)

Dear Committee Members,

I am sorry for sending you this report so close to the meeting. I was finishing some experiments, the results of which, I wanted to include in the report. I have attached the report as a word file. Please let me know if you have any trouble in opening the file.

Thank you.

Regards,
Saurav Pathria
PhD Student,
Dept of Biochemsitry,
University of Texas HSC,
San Antonio, TX

Subject: FW: 8-36 Comments from Reviewers

From: Pathria, Saurav (Pathria@uthscsa.edu)

To: saurav_pathria@yahoo.com;

Date: Wednesday, February 29, 2012 10:21 AM

Saurav Pathria
PhD Student,
Dept of Biochemsitry,
University of Texas HSC,
San Antonio, TX

From: Pathria, Saurav
Sent: Tuesday, December 13, 2011 3:38 PM
To: Serwer, Philip
Subject: 8-36 Comments from Reviewers

Dear Dr. Serwer,

I saw the comments from the reviewers on the 8-36 manuscript. I think a lot of things which they are suggesting is correct. We have not done an actual experiment to prove certain things. This paper is based on more assumptions than facts shown by data. I think, the isolation and mapping of deletion mutants is painstaking compared to the information that we get out of it.

In my opinion, we need to change the idea of the paper. It definitely made more sense with additional data but the data is not in a very good shape. The fluroscence microscopic image is out of focus and it is very hard to interpret anything based on that image whereas EM images are just fantastic. Ofcourse, I understand the reason for which you have put that image there, but reviewers seem to be very critical about the quality here which I think is a good course of action on their part.

I think we have to stop overassuming the 'phage-as-biofilm' hypothesis and just write what we think is going on as supported by the data (informatics). If, I was to write this paper then I would have just included the facts and informatics along with it. This paper is more informatically and genomically oriented so I guess my choice of a journal would have been something like 'Genome Research'. In informatics paper you come to conclusions based on informatics as no wet lab experiment is done in that. I have even seen informatics papers in 'Bacteriophage' with no real experiment done as all the data is generated in-silico.

One reviewer is right in saying that these are unrelated events. I can believe that translocation operon would transfer DNA from one cell to the other when host is propagating as a biofilm but I don't understand the reason that why would the phage start to propagate as a biofilm? You might have a pretty good explanation for it and if you don't then it is my request that we should take this hypothesis out of the paper.

I don't want people to read this paper and get super confused. We should say less or change the journal and send this manuscript to an 'informatically friendly' one.

These are my suggestions and I thank you for trying to get me a first author full paper by adding some additional data to complete the story but if doesn't work then I would say let us send it to 'Genome Research' as I am not in favour of trimming the informatics data (which is very important and I have spend considerable amount of time on it along with Dr. Hardies).

Thank you.

Regards,
Saurav Pathria
PhD Student,
Dept of Biochemsitry,
University of Texas HSC,
San Antonio, TX

Subject: FW: Hi

From: Pathria, Saurav (Pathria@uthscsa.edu)

To: saurav_pathria@yahoo.com;

Date: Tuesday, February 28, 2012 12:38 PM

Saurav Pathria
PhD Student,
Dept of Biochemsitry,
University of Texas HSC,
San Antonio, TX

From: Serwer, Philip
Sent: Friday, December 23, 2011 4:42 AM
To: Pathria, Saurav
Subject: RE: Hi

Dear Saurav:
I have not been at the UTHSCSA for the last week, but I will be in today.
Philip Serwer

From: Pathria, Saurav
Sent: Thursday, December 22, 2011 1:53 PM
To: Serwer, Philip
Subject: Hi

Dear Dr. Serwer,

I found a trashbin stuck in front of our lab door today and I also saw a light on. I turned the lights off
yesterday and there was no trashbin sitting in front of the door. I believe you me and Elena have the key
to the lab and housekeeping also has it. I almost fell when I opened the door today. I am sure someone
else with less athleticism would have banged the head on the cabinet. I thought I would ask you and
Elena first, if by mistake you or Elena did put that there. If neither of you visited the lab then I will be
getting in touch with the incharge of the housekeeping.

You have a wonderful Christmas and a very Happy New Year. I will see you in the New Year.

Thank you.

Regards,

Saurav Pathria
PhD Student,
Dept of Biochemsitry,
University of Texas HSC,
San Antonio, TX

Subject: FW: Manuscript +

From: Pathria, Saurav (Pathria@uthscsa.edu)

To: saurav_pathria@yahoo.com;

Date: Thursday, March 8, 2012 12:18 PM

Saurav Pathria
PhD Student,
Dept of Biochemsitry,
University of Texas HSC,
San Antonio, TX

From: Pathria, Saurav
Sent: Tuesday, March 06, 2012 11:43 AM
To: anthonys@jeffdavislawfirm.com
Subject: FW: Manuscript +

Please see the contradiction here. First he is saying it as holidays and then he is saying the department is open.

Saurav Pathria
PhD Student,
Dept of Biochemsitry,
University of Texas HSC,
San Antonio, TX

From: Serwer, Philip
Sent: Tuesday, December 27, 2011 11:13 AM
To: Pathria, Saurav
Subject: Re: Manuscript +

Dear Saurav:
Tuesday means today. The department is open and I am here until 5:00 PM. We have about 10 days to resubmit, which will make waiting until next week very risky.
Philip Serwer

From: "Pathria, Saurav" <Pathria@uthscsa.edu>
Date: Mon, 26 Dec 2011 23:40:41 -0600
To: Phillip Serwer <serwer@uthscsa.edu>
Subject: RE: Manuscript +

Dear Dr. Serwer,

I have some suggestions regarding your responses, which I will let you know next week. You are not going to send these responses this week, are you? By Tuesday and Wednesday, you mean of the next week, right? I have already finished working on the figure, but I can show you when you are also there, since you might have some suggestions and I will have to work on it real time.
                                   Regarding complementation, so far I have made fresh seed stocks of the amber 10, since the previous ones were not very good any more. They gave higher titers on the

non-permissive. The new seed stocks have 10^4 difference on the permissive and non-permissive just like my previous seed stocks. I am planning to run both 1D and 2D at the same time, so that I will get a little hands on training with 2D, before I do it with the mutants. I will have to check Elena's schedule for next week so that I can learn 2D from her.

Thank you.

Regards,
Saurav Pathria
PhD Student,
Dept of Biochemsitry,
University of Texas HSC,
San Antonio, TX

From: Serwer, Philip
Sent: Monday, December 26, 2011 3:55 PM
To: Pathria, Saurav
Subject: Manuscript +

Dear Saurav:

I hope that your holiday time is going well.

Although I am not completely finished with the revisions of the manuscript, I am close enough to send them, so that you can make whatever comments you think appropriate. Also, you can see where the new panel for Figure 3 fits. So, please have that panel ready on Tuesday.

I have attached (1) a draft of a response letter with the letter from the editor embedded in it, (2) the original manuscript as downloaded from the journal's website and (3) a draft of the revised manuscript. Revisions are indicated in red in both (1) and (3).

By Wednesday, please also have ready your data on the percentage of phage from your "complementation"-produced plaques that are wild type.

Philip Serwer

Subject: FW: Hi

From: Pathria, Saurav (Pathria@uthscsa.edu)

To: anthonys@jeffdavislawfirm.com;

Cc: saurav_pathria@yahoo.com;

Date: Tuesday, March 6, 2012 11:45 AM

He was insisting me to work on the holidays and did not want to ruin my plan for the holidays. There is another employee (A US citizen) who was on holidays.

Saurav Pathria
PhD Student,
Dept of Biochemsitry,
University of Texas HSC,
San Antonio, TX

From: Serwer, Philip
Sent: Thursday, December 29, 2011 3:54 PM
To: Pathria, Saurav
Subject: Re: Hi

Dear Saurav:
First of all, I am not too happy about being "stiffed". Second of all, I am not happy about the fact that, like just about everything else, getting the frame series of the video is encountering problems caused by lack of focus and initiative on your part. I should not have to tell you that the frames all have to be at the same magnification. I should not have to tell you that you might have to either talk to somebody or go to the web to get software.
The overall picture is that, as I said before, the rate of progress is much too slow. We are now at risk of not re-submitting the manuscript by the original deadline. So, please have (1) the frame series, correctly done with initiative to solve any problems that occur, and (2) a copy of the movie on a flash drive, by Monday at noon.
Philip Serwer

From: "Pathria, Saurav" <Pathria@uthscsa.edu>
Date: Wed, 28 Dec 2011 00:44:10 -0600
To: Phillip Serwer <serwer@uthscsa.edu>
Subject: Hi

Dear Dr. Serwer,

I will be out of San Antonio tomorrow and maybe rest of the week. I don't want to ruin the plans which I have already made for these holidays. The figure needs minor grooming, which I can do on Monday and the facility where the image is going to be processed will also be open by then.

Regards,
Saurav Pathria
PhD Student,
Dept of Biochemsitry,
University of Texas HSC,
San Antonio, TX

http://us.mg4.mail.yahoo.com/neo/launch?.rand=67fo2epuvahh3   5/25/2012

Subject: FW: 8-36 dimer frames

From: Pathria, Saurav (Pathria@uthscsa.edu)

To: saurav_pathria@yahoo.com;

Date: Wednesday, February 29, 2012 10:19 AM

Saurav Pathria
PhD Student,
Dept of Biochemsitry,
University of Texas HSC,
San Antonio, TX

From: Pathria, Saurav
Sent: Monday, January 02, 2012 1:23 PM
To: Serwer, Philip
Subject: 8-36 dimer frames

Dear Dr. Serwer,

Please see the attachment.

Regards,
Saurav Pathria
PhD Student,
Dept of Biochemsitry,
University of Texas HSC,
San Antonio, TX

RE: Academic Probation & Fall Semester grades for Research

Neal Robinson [robinson@uthscsa.edu]

Sent: Friday, January 20, 2012 2:04 PM
To: Pathria, Saurav
Cc: Serwer, Philip
Attachments: 2012-01-20 Pathria Academi~1.pdf (97 KB)

Dear Saurav,

Unfortunately, I must inform you that as of today the Biochemistry
Committee on Graduate Studies (COGS) is placing you on academic
probation in the Biochemistry Ph.D. program. The reasons for this
action are clearly stated in the attached letter. I have also placed a
copy of this letter in your Biochemistry mail box.

Please correct these deficiencies as soon as possible. If these
academic deficiencies remain at the end of Spring Semester, 2012, your
academic record will be reviewed by COGS for possible dismissal from the
Biochemistry Graduate Ph.D. program.
Sincerely,--

Neal C. Robinson, Ph.D.
Chair of Biochemistry COGS
Dept of Biochemistry MC 7760
The Univ Texas Health Sci Center
San Antonio, TX 78229-3900
(210) 567-3754

Subject:	FW: Bacteria with cloned gp10 of different types
From:	Pathria, Saurav (Pathria@uthscsa.edu)
To:	saurav_pathria@yahoo.com;
Date:	Tuesday, February 28, 2012 12:37 PM

Saurav Pathria
PhD Student,
Dept of Biochemsitry,
University of Texas HSC,
San Antonio, TX

From: Serwer, Philip
Sent: Wednesday, January 25, 2012 3:12 PM
To: Pathria, Saurav
Subject: FW: Bacteria with cloned gp10 of different types

Saurav:
As a reference, the text below is what I sent Elena for testing for transfer of mutations to a viable T3 phage.
Philip Serwer

From: Phillip Serwer <serwer@uthscsa.edu>
Date: Fri, 13 Jan 2012 16:46:29 -0600
To: "Wright, Elena T" <WRIGHTE@uthscsa.edu>
Cc: "Pathria, Saurav" <Pathria@uthscsa.edu>
Subject: Bacteria with cloned gp10 of different types

Elena:
I have talked to Saurav about the bacteria with cloned gp10. He has three. One has a single mutation in gene 10, one has two gene 10 mutations and one has a his-tag at the C-terminus of gene 10. The idea is to plate T3 amber mutant in gene 10 on each of these hosts, while using antibiotic (kanamycin) to be sure that the bacteria do not lose the cloned gene. The plaques might have primarily the amber mutant and wild type revertant phage in them. But, with a little luck, the cloned gene will transfer and some of the phages that can now plate without the amber suppressor (i.e., plate on E. coli BB/1 or BL21) will have received the cloned gene. These phages hopefully be recognizable because they have either unusual or temperature sensitive plating.

So, the idea is to do the following with the plaques formed on each of the hosts with a cloned gene.

(1) First, simply remove a well separated plaque, resuspend in T7 buffer and then plate on 0-11' (everything is likely to plate) and also on either BB/1 or BL21 (only revertants and possibly phage with transferred genes plate).

(2) If the level of platers on non-suppressors is above 1/100 of the level on 0-11', then pick 2-3 plaques, resuspend in T7 buffer and plate at two temperatures on the non-suppressor: 28°C and 39 °C. If growth occurs at one temperature, but not the other (even if the growth is different from wild type at either temperature), freeze the plaque and tell me. This could be a phage that has received gene 10 from the host. In the case of the his-tagged gene, Saurav has an antibody-based technique that can be used to detect the his tag in a plaque.

Philip Serwer

PS: If anyone sees a problem with this scheme, please let me know right away.

Subject: FW: Manuscript

From: Pathria, Saurav (Pathria@uthscsa.edu)

To: saurav_pathria@yahoo.com;

Date: Monday, March 26, 2012 9:59 AM

Saurav Pathria
PhD Student,
Dept of Biochemsitry,
University of Texas HSC,
San Antonio, TX

From: Pathria, Saurav
Sent: Thursday, January 26, 2012 1:06 PM
To: Serwer, Philip
Subject: RE: Manuscript

OK.

Saurav Pathria
PhD Student,
Dept of Biochemsitry,
University of Texas HSC,
San Antonio, TX

From: Serwer, Philip
Sent: Thursday, January 26, 2012 1:05 PM
To: Pathria, Saurav
Subject: Re: Manuscript

Dear Saurav:
The first sub-section of the Discussion Section covers the potential deletion of genes during laboratory
propagation in the absence "of selection for stability to elevated temperature". This deletion is expected
to occur, although more slowly. Generally, mutations occur at random, as shown in numerous studies,
although, in a few systems, some studies have suggested that some mutations are themselves under
genetic control. We have nothing to contribute on this latter point, based on the data presented.
I plan to re-submit either late today or tomorrow.
Philip Serwer

From: "Pathria, Saurav" <Pathria@uthscsa.edu>
Date: Thu, 26 Jan 2012 12:54:58 -0600
To: Phillip Serwer <serwer@uthscsa.edu>
Subject: RE: Manuscript

Dear Dr. Serwer,

I think the revision and your responses are nice. I only have one major comment, if these genes are non-
essential under laboratory conditions then what we call as wild type should shed these genes during

propagation as well. But, it does not. These genes are shed by the phage only under stringent conditions.

Also, we don't know why it would shed some genes in one scenario and others in different scenario and no gene in another, under the same stringent conditions and why not all of these together. We can add this in the text if you want, as it would make this study interesting for someone studying genome dynamics. The key question is that is there a factor which determines the genes to be deleted or is it just random. We know it is temperature and EDTA in our case to some extent and can we actually see all of these cellular homologs getting deleted from the genome if we increase the temperature even further without killing the phage.

These are some unanswered intriguing questions. We can write this as to where this study could be taken in the future, if you want.

Regards,
Saurav Pathria
PhD Student,
Dept of Biochemsitry,
University of Texas HSC,
San Antonio, TX

From: Serwer, Philip
Sent: Wednesday, January 25, 2012 4:47 PM
To: Pathria, Saurav
Cc: Hardies, Stephen C
Subject: Manuscript

Saurav:
I have attached a complete draft of (1) a second revision of the manuscript and (2) a response letter. I will be checking both texts for the next day or two. Please check the references and data (and anything else that you want to check) to be sure that all is in order. I must re-submit by Friday or the re-submission is likely to be delayed for over two weeks. So, it is important to work quickly.
I note that the only major change is the delay of discussion of the biofilm hypothesis until the Discussion Section. The rest is minor, as both the editor and the referee indicate directly. Essentially no change has been made in the informatics sections. Changes from the first revision are in red; changes from the second revision are in blue.
Philip Serwer

Subject: FW: Good News

From: Pathria, Saurav (Pathria@uthscsa.edu)

To: saurav_pathria@yahoo.com;

Date: Wednesday, February 29, 2012 12:51 PM

Saurav Pathria
PhD Student,
Dept of Biochemsitry,
University of Texas HSC,
San Antonio, TX

From: William Haldenwang [haldenwang@uthscsa.edu]
Sent: Wednesday, February 08, 2012 11:40 AM
To: Pathria, Saurav
Subject: Re: Good News

Really good Saurav!!

William Haldenwang
Dept. Microbiology & Immunology
UTHSCSA
7703 Floyd Curl Dr.
San Antonio, TX 78229-3950

----- Original Message -----
From: Pathria, Saurav
To: Haldenwang, William G ; Weintraub, Susan E ; Hardies, Stephen C ; Serwer, Philip
Sent: Wednesday, February 08, 2012 11:25 AM
Subject: Good News

Dear Committee Members,

I am very delighted to inform you that I have isolated a T3 phage in which two Glutamines at position 8 and 9 have been mutated to Alanines in gene 10 (major capsid protein) by recombination event. I have also revised the procedure where I can see capsid I, capsid II and fully assembled phage particles on a one dimensional gel.

Thank you.

Regards,
Saurav Pathria
PhD Student,
Dept of Biochemsitry,
University of Texas HSC,
San Antonio, TX

Subject: FW: Good News

From: Pathria, Saurav (Pathria@uthscsa.edu)

To: saurav_pathria@yahoo.com;

Date: Wednesday, February 29, 2012 12:42 PM

Saurav Pathria
PhD Student,
Dept of Biochemsitry,
University of Texas HSC,
San Antonio, TX

From: Stephen C. Hardies [hardres@uthscsa.edu]
Sent: Wednesday, February 08, 2012 1:37 PM
To: Pathria, Saurav
Subject: Re: Good News

Saurav:

That sounds like some serious progress.

Steve Hardies

> Dear Committee Members,
>
>
>
> I am very delighted to inform you that I have isolated a T3 phage in which
> two Glutamines at position 8 and 9 have been mutated to Alanines in gene
> 10 (major capsid protein) by recombination event. I have also revised the
> procedure where I can see capsid I, capsid II and fully assembled phage
> particles on a one dimensional gel.
>
>
>
> Thank you.
>
>
>
> Regards,
>
> Saurav Pathria
> PhD Student,
> Dept of Biochemsitry,
> University of Texas HSC,
> San Antonio, TX
>

Subject:	FW: Good News
From:	Pathria, Saurav (Pathria@uthscsa.edu)
To:	saurav_pathria@yahoo.com;
Date:	Wednesday, February 29, 2012 12:52 PM

Saurav Pathria
PhD Student,
Dept of Biochemsitry,
University of Texas HSC,
San Antonio, TX

From: Weintraub, Susan E
Sent: Wednesday, February 08, 2012 11:26 AM
To: Pathria, Saurav; Haldenwang, William G; Hardies, Stephen C; Serwer, Philip
Subject: RE: Good News

Dear Saurav,

Thanks for letting us know the good news.

Regards,

Sue Weintraub

******
Susan T. Weintraub, Ph.D.
Professor, Department of Biochemistry
Director, Mass Spectrometry Laboratory
The University of Texas Health Science Center
   at San Antonio
7703 Floyd Curl Drive
MC 7760
San Antonio, Texas 78229-3900
(210) 567-4013
(210) 567-5524 (fax)
weintraub@uthscsa.edu

From: Pathria, Saurav
Sent: Wednesday, February 08, 2012 11:25 AM
To: Haldenwang, William G; Weintraub, Susan E; Hardies, Stephen C; Serwer, Philip
Subject: Good News

Dear Committee Members,

I am very delighted to inform you that I have isolated a T3 phage in which two Glutamines at position 8 and 9 have been mutated to Alanines in gene 10 (major capsid protein) by recombination event. I have also revised the procedure where I can see capsid I, capsid II and fully assembled phage particles on a one dimensional gel.

Thank you.

Regards,
Saurav Pathria
PhD Student,
Dept of Biochemsitry,
University of Texas HSC,
San Antonio, TX

Subject: FW: Your Academic Probation

From: Pathria, Saurav (Pathria@uthscsa.edu)

To: saurav_pathria@yahoo.com;

Date: Monday, February 27, 2012 10:20 AM

Saurav Pathria
PhD Student,
Dept of Biochemsitry,
University of Texas HSC,
San Antonio, TX

From: Neal Robinson [robinson@uthscsa.edu]
Sent: Monday, February 27, 2012 10:03 AM
To: Pathria, Saurav
Subject: Re: Your Academic Probation

Dear Saurav,

I am sorry that you took my letter as a personal criticism of you. It
is my duty as chair of COGS to inform you of your status in the
program. Because you are delinquent on submitting your dissertation
proposal, and because your dissertation committee has given you a grade
of unsatisfactory, it is my responsibility to inform you that you are on
academic probation. Your committee met and decided what you needed to
accomplish this semester to once again be in good academic standing.
They thought it best that I be informed of their decision and asked me
to inform you of their requirements. For that reason, I sent you the
letter of last week.

The role of COGS in probationary process is to inform students of their
academic status. We do not participate directly in the remediation
process - that is up to the class instructor, the dissertation
committee, and/or supervising professor depending upon the reason for
academic probation. If the student is unable to return to good academic
standing, or receives another grade of C, or U it is the COGS
responsibility to review the students progress and record to determine
if they should continue in the program. In your case, this would not
happen unless you received another grade of Unsatisfactory for Spring
semester, or if you failed to submit your dissertation proposal, which
was due 14 months ago.

As far as meeting with me, I am more than happy to meet with you at any
time you desire. I always have an open door policy and many students
take advantage of it to come and discuss graduate program issues. If
you would like to meet with me, please let me know a convenient time and
I will meet you in my office.

Sincerely,
Neal Robinson
Chair Biochemistry COGS

.On 2/24/2012 5:09 PM, Pathria, Saurav wrote:
> Dear Dr. Robinson,
>
> First of all, I am very disappointed that being my Graduate Advisor you have not even talked to me once about this and you have send me this long e-mail with set of goals to be achieved in a specific amount of time. I have spend significant amount of my last semester's time on 0305phi8-36 phage manuscript preparation and bioinformatics related with it. Along with the completion of this manuscript, I worked on a procedure which I established on my own as no procedure like such existed in our lab before this. The dissertation proposal that I presented in front of the department, got my full attention in this semester because in last semester 8-36 paper kept popping up in between my experiments. Inspite of these two tasks, I made significant progress on my dissertation in last semester as I generated three mutants. Also, the manuscript on which I spend a lot of my last semester's time is published by god's grace and I am the first author on it. But, so far I have not heard a single word of appreciation from anyone. Rather, I have been mentally pressurized. So, I don't know why I got an unsatisfactory in the last semester at first place.
>
> In this semester I have made a phage with mutant gene 10 which in itself is a very big deal. I had to struggle a lot with the whole procedure because some of the best groups have published papers in which they have used complementation procedure which is absolutely wrong. To address that issue and get the correct scientific information out, I wrote a manuscript, but somehow it was not much appreciated because those are some big names. Anyways, that is not my purpose of writing. My purpose is that you have to put forward targets which are achievable.
>
> If President Obama tells NASA that you have to send a person to Mars in three months or you all will be fired then the most possible outcome will that there will not be a single person working in NASA anymore.
>
> So, if you are going to continue this practise then please accept this e-mail as my resignation from the program.
>
> Thank you.
>
> Regards,
> Saurav Pathria
> PhD Student,
> Dept of Biochemsitry,
> University of Texas HSC,
> San Antonio, TX
>
> From: Neal Robinson [robinson@uthscsa.edu]
> Sent: Friday, February 24, 2012 4:19 PM
> To: Pathria, Saurav
> Cc: Serwer, Philip
> Subject: RE: Your Academic Probation

>
> Dear Saurav,
>
> On January 20th I informed you that you were being placed on Academic
> Probation for your unsatisfactory progress towards the Ph.D. degree
> requirements of the Department of Biochemistry. Unless your committee
> decides that you have met the minimum standards expected by a graduate
> student in the Biochemistry Ph.D. program by the end of Spring semester,
> your progress will be reviewed by the Biochemistry Graduate Program by
> the Biochemistry Committee on Graduate Studies (COGS), with possible
> dismissal from the Biochemistry Ph.D. program. Your dissertation
> committee has established some minimum standards that you must achieve
> this semester. Therefore, removal of your probationary status is
> contingent upon three requirements that are described in detail in the
> attached letter. A copy of this letter has also placed in your
> departmental mail box.
>
> Sincerely,
>
> --
> Neal C. Robinson
> Chair, Biochemistry COGS
> Dept of Biochemistry MC 7760
> The Univ Texas Health Sci Center
> San Antonio, TX 78229-3900
> (210) 567-3754
>

--
Neal C. Robinson
Dept of Biochemistry MC 7760
The Univ Texas Health Sci Center
San Antonio, TX 78229-3900
(210) 567-3754

Subject: FW: Your Academic Probation

From: Pathria, Saurav (Pathria@uthscsa.edu)

To: saurav_pathria@yahoo.com;

Date: Tuesday, February 28, 2012 12:33 PM

Saurav Pathria
PhD Student,
Dept of Biochemsitry,
University of Texas HSC,
San Antonio, TX

From: Pathria, Saurav
Sent: Tuesday, February 28, 2012 11:54 AM
To: Weiss, David
Subject: FW: Your Academic Probation

Dear Dr. Weiss,

I copied you this e-mail on February 24, 2012. The reason for my sending you this e-mail was that I was unneccesarily 'bullied' and 'harassed' by my supervisor. My supervisor Dr. Philip Serwer has many times 'blackmailed' and threatened me that since I am an international student, he has the power to cancel my visa anytime, so I should work like crazy. I did as he said, I worked very hard, including weekends and holidays but he somehow took this thing as granted and his demands kept on increasing day by day.
I have passed all my courses, passed my qualifier and I am a PhD candidate, despite this he blackmailed me that he will give me a Master's and not a PhD. I have also published a first author paper and some of my committee members are my supervisor's close collaborators and dance to his tune and give grades to me, what he tells them to. I am really frustrated by all this now. I have seen Biochemistry awarding degrees to students who had no paper published and not a lot of data in their dissertation either. I just entered my fifth year of the PhD program this semester and no one is looking at my publication and continuosly threatening me for a dismissal. No one can work in these conditions.
I came here all the way from India, for a PhD. I know, I have done sufficient work in the research. If you could consider my request and personally take this case into your own hands and solve it then it would be great, otherwise I am going to take my case to the court in 2-3 days.

Thank you.

Regards,
Saurav Pathria
PhD Student,
Dept of Biochemsitry,
University of Texas HSC,
San Antonio, TX

From: Pathria, Saurav

Sent: Friday, February 24, 2012 5:09 PM
To: Robinson, Neal C
Cc: Serwer, Philip; Hardies, Stephen C; Weintraub, Susan E; Haldenwang, William G; Nicholson, Bruce J; Weiss, David
Subject: RE: Your Academic Probation

Dear Dr. Robinson,

First of all, I am very disappointed that being my Graduate Advisor you have not even talked to me once about this and you have send me this long e-mail with set of goals to be achieved in a specific amount of time. I have spend significant amount of my last semester's time on 0305phi8-36 phage manuscript preparation and bioinformatics related with it. Along with the completion of this manuscript, I worked on a procedure which I established on my own as no procedure like such existed in our lab before this. The dissertation proposal that I presented in front of the department, got my full attention in this semester because in last semester 8-36 paper kept popping up in between my experiments. Inspite of these two tasks, I made significant progress on my dissertation in last semester as I generated three mutants. Also, the manuscript on which I spend a lot of my last semester's time is published by god's grace and I am the first author on it. But, so far I have not heard a single word of appreciation from anyone. Rather, I have been mentally pressurized. So, I don't know why I got an unsatisfactory in the last semester at first place.

In this semester I have made a phage with mutant gene 10 which in itself is a very big deal. I had to struggle a lot with the whole procedure because some of the best groups have published papers in which they have used complementation procedure which is absolutely wrong. To address that issue and get the correct scientific information out, I wrote a manuscript, but somehow it was not much appreciated because those are some big names. Anyways, that is not my purpose of writing. My purpose is that you have to put forward targets which are achievable.

If President Obama tells NASA that you have to send a person to Mars in three months or you all will be fired then the most possible outcome will that there will not be a single person working in NASA anymore.

So, if you are going to continue this practise then please accept this e-mail as my resignation from the program.

Thank you.

Regards,
Saurav Pathria
PhD Student,
Dept of Biochemsitry,
University of Texas HSC,
San Antonio, TX

From: Neal Robinson [robinson@uthscsa.edu]
Sent: Friday, February 24, 2012 4:19 PM
To: Pathria, Saurav
Cc: Serwer, Philip
Subject: RE: Your Academic Probation

Dear Saurav,

On January 20th I informed you that you were being placed on Academic Probation for your unsatisfactory progress towards the Ph.D. degree requirements of the Department of Biochemistry. Unless your committee decides that you have met the minimum standards expected by a graduate student in the Biochemistry Ph.D. program by the end of Spring semester, your progress will be reviewed by the Biochemistry Graduate Program by the Biochemistry Committee on Graduate Studies (COGS), with possible dismissal from the Biochemistry Ph.D. program. Your dissertation committee has established some minimum standards that you must achieve this semester. Therefore, removal of your probationary status is contingent upon three requirements that are described in detail in the attached letter. A copy of this letter has also placed in your departmental mail box.

Sincerely,

--
Neal C. Robinson
Chair, Biochemistry COGS
Dept of Biochemistry MC 7760
The Univ Texas Health Sci Center
San Antonio, TX 78229-3900
(210) 567-3754

RE: Spring semester class registration

Pathria, Saurav
Sent: Tuesday, December 06, 2011 12:54 PM
To: Robinson, Neal C

Dear Dr. Robinson,

I have not submitted my dissertation proposal yet. My committee has not got back to me for past 6 months since I submitted by proposal to them. I am not sure what to do in situations like these. How many semesters before we have to submit our proposal in order to graduate?

Also, I am trying to enroll for Spring 2012 semester, I could see BIOC 6097, but no BIOC 6069. I believe, I have to enroll for 8 units of BIOC 6097 and 1 unit of BIOC 6069. Do you need to give me permission for enrolling in BIOC 6069?

Thank you.

Regards,
Saurav Pathria
PhD Student,
Dept of Biochemsitry,
University of Texas HSC,
San Antonio, TX

From: Neal Robinson [robinson@uthscsa.edu]
Sent: Monday, November 21, 2011 2:00 PM
To: Chen, Hongzhi; Garg, Neha; Li, Mengyao; Pathria, Saurav; Ullevig, Sarah Lynn; Villarreal, Maria Magdalena
Subject: Spring semester class registration

Biochemistry Graduate Students,

I've given both of you permission to enroll in Research for Spring semester. For those of you who have successfully submitted their Dissertation Proposal to the Graduate Dean's Office, I have also given you permission to enroll for 3 credits of Dissertation. If you need any other course permissions, please let me know.

Also a few reminders:
1. You MUST have your Fall Semester Committee meeting and give me your committee evaluation BEFORE I submit grades at the end of December. Otherwise, I will need to give you a grade of Unsatisfactory for Research and Scientific Writing.

2. If a majority of your committee, including your supervising professor, gives you a grade of Excellent, you will be excused from having the Spring Semester Committee meeting.

3. If a majority of your committee members gives you a grade of Unsatisfactory, you will need to remediate the grade of U, by having an additional committee meeting before the second week of February.

Neal Robinson
Chair of Biochemistry COGS

--
Neal C. Robinson
Dept of Biochemistry MC 7760
The Univ Texas Health Sci Center
San Antonio, TX 78229-3900
(210) 567-3754

Subject: FW: Note form COGS

From: Pathria, Saurav (Pathria@uthscsa.edu)

To: saurav_pathria@yahoo.com;

Date: Thursday, March 1, 2012 12:03 PM

Saurav Pathria
PhD Student,
Dept of Biochemsitry,
University of Texas HSC,
San Antonio, TX

From: Pathria, Saurav
Sent: Wednesday, February 29, 2012 10:45 PM
To: Robinson, Neal C
Cc: Nicholson, Bruce J; Serwer, Philip; Barnes, Larry D; Weiss, David
Subject: RE: Note form COGS

Dear Dr. Robinson,

Please see my e-mail below, which clearly shows that I was actively involved to get my proposal approved by the committee. After submitting my revised proposal on July 4 2011, I never heard back from the committee except Dr. Weintraub response, which is below. Being a student, I can only remind them which I did. As far as the graduate handbook is concerned, you can see in my e-mail below, I did mention about it to the committee. I also reminded you on December 6, 2011 that the committee has not yet got back to me regarding my proposal, but I did not get any response from you (if you need a copy of that e-mail, I can forward it to you).

                    I know members are very busy sometimes but such a long time to give a student feedback is way too much. These are the things which are out of a student's control.

Thank you.

Regards,
Saurav Pathria
PhD Student,
Dept of Biochemsitry,
University of Texas HSC,
San Antonio, TX

From: Weintraub, Susan E
Sent: Tuesday, October 18, 2011 3:28 PM
To: Pathria, Saurav; Hardies, Stephen C
Cc: Serwer, Philip; Haldenwang, William G
Subject: RE: Dissertation Proposal

Hi Saurav,

I will look at your proposal by the end of the week. I have several deadlines before then.

Regards,

http://us.mg4.mail.yahoo.com/neo/launch?.rand=67fo2epuvahh3   5/25/2012

Sue Weintraub

******

Susan T. Weintraub, Ph.D.
Professor, Department of Biochemistry
Director, Mass Spectrometry Laboratory
The University of Texas Health Science Center
   at San Antonio
7703 Floyd Curl Drive
MC 7760
San Antonio, Texas 78229-3900
(210) 567-4043
(210) 567-5524 (fax)
weintraub@uthscsa.edu

From: Pathria, Saurav
Sent: Tuesday, October 18, 2011 3:21 PM
To: Weintraub, Susan E; Hardies, Stephen C
Cc: Serwer, Philip; Haldenwang, William G
Subject: Dissertation Proposal

Dear Committee Members,

It has been nearly 4 months since I last sent you updated dissertation proposal. Even after my repeated request, I have still not heard back from you. Some of you had comments based on which I did make changes in the last draft that I sent you. I am already very late in submitting the dissertation proposal (according to our graduate handbook). I would appreciate if without any further delay you can approve it or if you have further comments send it back to me.

I look forward to hear from you soon.

Thank you.

Regards,
Saurav Pathria
PhD Student,
Dept of Biochemsitry,
University of Texas HSC,
San Antonio, TX

Saurav Pathria
PhD Student,
Dept of Biochemsitry,
University of Texas HSC,
San Antonio, TX

From: Neal Robinson [robinson@uthscsa.edu]
Sent: Wednesday, February 29, 2012 6:07 PM
To: Pathria, Saurav
Cc: Nicholson, Bruce J; Serwer, Philip; Barnes, Larry D
Subject: Note form COGS

Dear Saurav,

I'm writing to reiterate the importance of you meeting with me regarding the difficulties you are having in the Biochemistry Graduate Program. To date, you have not taken advantage of discussing your problems with me.

I also want to emphasize, that to date you are on academic probation, but this does NOT mean that you are being considered for dismissal from the Biochemistry Graduate Program. It is not unusual for students to be placed on academic probation, but normally their academic deficiencies are corrected within the next semester and they, therefore, return to good academic standing.

Description of Academic Probation (THE POLICY HANDBOOK for the BIOCHEMISTRY GRADUATE PROGRAM . p 10)
A student is placed on academic probation for failure to meet any of the requirements of the program. The Graduate Advisor notifies the student in writing the basis for the probation, the requirements to rectify the probation, and the time allowed to complete these requirements (usually one semester). A student on academic probation is not allowed to advance to candidacy. A student who fails to meet the probationary requirements, or who fails to satisfy a second requirement while on probation is subject to dismissal from the Ph.D. program. COGS may recommend to the Associate Dean of the Graduate School the dismissal of a student at any time for failure to make satisfactory progress. A majority vote of the members of COGS is required for a recommendation of dismissal.

It is, however, important for you to realize the seriousness of academic probation. As stated in the Handbook, If the academic deficiencies persist and you receive another unsatisfactory grade, your status in the graduate program will be reviewed the the Biochemistry Committee of Graduate Studies (COGS). At that time, COGS will decide whether you should continue in the program, or whether it recommends you be dismissed. In your case, COGS will review your status in the program ONLY IF you receive another unsatisfactory grade for Spring Semester, OR if you fail to submit your approved Dissertation Proposal to COGS for approval by the end of Spring Semester.

Your failure to complete the requirement of submitting your Dissertation Proposal to COGS by May, 2010 is, in itself, a very serious academic deficiency. I have attached the section of the THE POLICY HANDBOOK for the BIOCHEMISTRY GRADUATE PROGRAM that concerns the Dissertation Proposal (Page 15). It clearly states that you were to have submitted the proposal to COGS NO LATER THAN December, 2010. Failure to meet this deadline meant that you MUST have asked for approval from COGS to delay your submission, which you HAVE NOT DONE. You presented our Dissertation Proposal Seminar on May 2, 2011, which was already 5 months past the deadline. It is now 9 months later and you still have not submitted the approved proposal to COGS. Therefore, unless you correct this serious academic problem by the end of Spring Semester, 2012, YOU WILL BE CALLED BEFORE COGS to explain why you have not met this requirement.

All Ph.D. graduate students MUST meet the above mentioned Dissertation Proposal requirement to remain in the Graduate School of Biomedical Sciences. Not only must COGS approve the proposal, but it together with the composition of your Dissertation Committee MUST be submitted to the Graduate Dean's Office. Once this is done, you then MUST enroll for AT LEAST two semesters of Dissertation (BIOC 7099) to be eligible for graduation. This requirements was established for the benefit of the graduate students themselves. Unless the student can define a Ph.D. Dissertation Project by the end of the third year and have it approved by his Dissertation Committee, it would be impossible for the student to graduate within a reasonable length of time. You are now beginning your fifth year in the Ph.D. program and have yet to submit an approved proposal, your time line for graduation even if you have no other academic problems is going to be at least six years or longer. Such a slow rate of progress is clearly unacceptable.

--
Neal C. Robinson

Chair, Biochemistry COGS
Dept of Biochemistry MC 7760
The Univ Texas Health Sci Center
San Antonio, TX 78229-3900
(210) 567-3754

Subject:	FW: What is happening?
From:	Pathria, Saurav (Pathria@uthscsa.edu)
To:	weissd@uthscsa.edu;
Cc:	saurav_pathria@yahoo.com;
Date:	Thursday, March 8, 2012 5:17 PM

Dear Dr. Weiss,

I have received this e-mail from Dr. Serwer. I am not sure if you have intitiated an investigation of my complaint. I hope you understand that I have filed a complaint against my supervisor and committee. Also, Chair of graduate studies (Dr. Neal C. Robinson) has misused his powers. I fear a 'retaliation' from them, so ofcourse, due to 'hostile work environment', I can not resume work till you resolve this issue.

I look forward to hear from you soon.

Thank you.

Regards,
Saurav Pathria
PhD Student,
Dept of Biochemsitry,
University of Texas HSC,
San Antonio, TX

From: Serwer, Philip
Sent: Thursday, March 08, 2012 4:22 PM
To: Pathria, Saurav
Subject: What is happening?

Dear Saurav:
I have not seen you for a while. What is happening?
Philip Serwer

Subject: RE: Your Status

From: Nicholson, Bruce J (NicholsonB@uthscsa.edu)

To: BarnesL@uthscsa.edu; weissd@uthscsa.edu;

Cc: ROBINSON@uthscsa.edu; SERWER@uthscsa.edu; HALDENWANG@uthscsa.edu; HARDIES@uthscsa.edu; Weintraub@uthscsa.edu; saurav_pathria@yahoo.com;

Date: Monday, March 12, 2012 8:05 PM

Hi Larry

I was planning in writing to you to commend you on writing such a clear and concise summary of events and laying out Saurav's options. I guess you did achieve clarity, and Saurav has chosen his path of redress. I am confident that we have followed the spirit of the procedures of the graduate school throughout this case, and if anything, have only been guilty of giving him too much rope and exercising too much patience in this case, in the hope that he would ultimately figure out how to perform at a graduate level. I also completely agree that Dr. Robinson in this process has simply been interpreting and enforcing as well as he can the rules of the graduate school and recommendations of his committee, as he should be as Chair of COGS, and in no way has done anything inappropriate. In fact all of his recent actions were discussed with me beforehand and met with my full approval.

In terms of a practical response, we clearly need to consult with Jack Park or whoever the appropriate legal advisor is for this case. Given his litigious response, I would posit that his resignation per his previous letter be accepted forthwith, as he clearly does not intend to meet any of his committee's recommended courses of remediation. Under these conditions, Dr. Serwer would no longer serve as his advisor, and he would no longer receive support from the University. This would seem incongruous with a law suit in any event. In addition, should he for any reason persist in attempting to get his latest work published, he will not be able to submit it under the UTHSCSA name.

Please let me know if I can be of any assistance as this moves forward.

Bruce

Bruce J. Nicholson, Ph.D.
Professor and Chair of Biochemistry
University of Texas Health Science Center at San Antonio

Tel: 210-567-3772
Fax: 210-567-6595
e-mail: nicholsonb@uthscsa.edu

From: Pathria, Saurav
Sent: Monday, March 12, 2012 7:41 PM
To: Barnes, Larry D
Cc: Weiss, David; Nicholson, Bruce J; Robinson, Neal C; Serwer, Philip; Haldenwang, William G; Hardies, Stephen C; Weintraub, Susan E; ,
Subject: RE: Your Status

Dear Dr. Barnes,

I respectfully inform you that I have filed a lawsuit in the Bexar county district court for the issues that I was facing at the defendant The University of Texas Health Science Center at San Antonio, cause#2012CI04075.

I think this issue will have to be settled in the court of law.

Thank you.

Regards,
Saurav Pathria
PhD Student,
Dept of Biochemsitry,
University of Texas HSC,
San Antonio, TX

From: Barnes, Larry D
Sent: Monday, March 12, 2012 5:13 PM
To: Pathria, Saurav
Cc: Weiss, David; Nicholson, Bruce J; Robinson, Neal C; Serwer, Philip; Haldenwang, William G; Hardies, Stephen C; Weintraub, Susan E
Subject: Your Status

Dear Saurav,

Dr. Weiss forwarded your messages of March 8, February 28, and February 24, 2012 to me for follow up. I have reviewed email messages exchanged among you, Drs. Serwer, Weintraub, Hardies, Haldenwang, Robinson, Nicholson, and Weiss, and I have spoken with Drs. Weiss, Nicholson, Serwer, and Robinson.

My comments are:

> 1. Your message of March 8, 2012 to Dr. Weiss states: "I am not sure if you have initiated an investigation of my complaint. I hope you understand that I have filed a complaint against my supervisor and committee. Also, Chair of graduate studies (Dr. Neal C. Robinson) has misused his powers."
>
> Presumably, you are referring to your message of February 28, 2012 to Dr. Weiss, although you do not formally state that you are filing a complaint against your supervisor and committee. Also, there is no mention of Dr. Robinson in this particular message.
>
> Thus, you should consider my responses in this message as an informal investigation into your informal complaint.
>
> 2. You state in your message of March 8, 2012 to Dr. Weiss that: "Also, Chair of graduate studies (Dr. Neal C. Robinson) has misused his powers."
>
> Dr. Robinson has not misused his powers. He has been executing his responsibilities as Chair of the Committee on Graduate Studies and as graduate advisor in the Biochemistry graduate program.
>
> His formal letter (and related email) to you on January 20, 2012 explicitly states that you are on academic probation and the reasons for the probation, and he cites the relevant

policies in the handbook for the Biochemistry graduate program. His letter also states the consequences if you fail to address the deficiencies in the Spring 2012 semester. Clearly, a "U" grade in Research (BIOC 6097) for the Fall, 2011 semester and the failure to submit an approved dissertation research proposal by the end of your fourth year in the graduate program are definite reasons for academic probation and are indicators of inadequate academic progress for a student in the 5th year.

Dr. Robinson's formal letter (and related email) to you on February 24, 2012 re-iterates that you are on academic probation. His letter also explicitly states what your supervising committee requires you to satisfactorily complete in the Spring, 2012 semester in order to be removed from academic probation. Thus, Dr. Robinson did not impose these requirements himself, but was re-stating the requirements set forth by your committee. He provided this information "…to assist you in removing your probationary status".

3. In your email message to Dr. Robinson on February 24, 2012 in response to his letter and message to you on the same day, you summarize how you spent your time in the fall 2011 semester and how you have spent your time so far this semester. You also state that: "Anyways, that is not my purpose of writing. My purpose is that you have to put forward targets which are achievable." "So, if you are going to continue this practice then please accept this e-mail as my resignation from the program."

I emphasize that Dr. Robinson did not set the targets. He was, as noted above, re-stating the requirements set forth by your committee. He has the responsibility as COGS chair to "…continue this practice…" of informing students of their academic status and the conditions relevant to that status.

Since you state in your message: "…**please accept this e-mail as my resignation from the program**.", it is unclear the intent of your email messages after February 24, 2012 since you resigned from the program.

Please contact me so we can arrange a time to discuss this matter **in person**. I am currently available most of the time on March 13, 14, 19-21st. **If I do not hear from you by 5:00 pm on March 21, 2012, I will accept your above statement of resignation as final, and we will initiate the requisite paperwork.**

Regards,
Larry D. Barnes

Larry D. Barnes
Associate Dean
Office of the Graduate Dean
University of Texas Health Science Center
San Antonio, TX 78229-3900
P: (210) 567-3711
F: (210) 567-3719
barnesl@uthscsa.edu

June 9, 2009

To whom it may concern:

This is to verify that Mr. Saurav Pathria is a teaching assistant in the Department of Biochemistry and works in my laboratory in Department of Biochemsitry, The University of Texas Health Science Center at San Antonio, is in good academic standing. Mr. Saurav Pathria is currently working on the project "Genetics of bacteriophage 0305phi-8-36" and is employed at the UTHSCSA for the period of 01/07/2008 to 08/31/2013 with an annual salary of $ 26000/-.

Sincerely,

(signature)

Dr. Philip Serwer, PhD
Professor
Department of Biochemsitry
(210) 567-3765

(signature)

Dr. Bruce J. Nicholson, PhD
Professor and Chairman
Department of Biochemistry
(210) 567-3772

The University of Texas
Health Science Center at San Antonio
Mail Code 7971
7703 Floyd Curl Drive
San Antonio, Texas 78229-3900

Office of International Services

(210) 567-6241
FAX: (210) 567-6240

May 14, 2007

Dear Mr. Pathria,

Congratulations on your acceptance to The University of Texas health Science Center at San Antonio (UTHSCSA). Enclosed is a Certificate of Eligibility for Nonimmigrant Student (SEVIS Form I-20)

In order to obtain your Nonimmigrant Student "F" Visa, you should present the enclosed SEVIS Form I-20, passport, and visa application at the nearest United States Consulate. The F-1 Visa will be stamped in your passport. Your passport and I-20 will then be returned to you. Upon your arrival in the United States, you will be required to present your passport, visa and the I-20 to the Immigration Officer at the port of entry. **Please ensure that the officer stamps your I-20 and I-94 Admission/Departure record that you are an "F-1" admitted for "D/S" (Duration of Status). Please make sure that both documents are returned to you after they have been stamped.**

You are required to arrive **NO LATER THAN THE <u>PROGRAM START DATE</u> ON YOUR I-20. If you are going to arrive later YOU MUST NOTIFY YOUR DEPARTMENT AND OUR OFFICE <u>IN ADVANCE</u>.** Arriving late will jeopardize your entrance into the U.S.A. and your status. Also, you may not enter the U.S.A. 30 days earlier than the program beginning date.

The University of Texas Health Science Center at San Antonio, in issuing this certificate, assumes responsibilities in relation to your stay in the United States. It is therefore important that you conform to all applicable rules and regulations of the U.S. Department of Homeland Security while you are in this country.

IMPORTANT!!!!
1) **If you changed your travel date and received more than one I-20, you MUST USE THE NEW I-20 WITH UPDATED START DATE TO ENTER THE U.S. Also, you must return your old I-20(s) to Office of International Services by express mail immediately after you receive the new I-20.** Our address is 7703 Floyd Curl Dr. MC7971, San Antonio, TX 78229-3990 U.S.A.
2) **Once you have arrived to our campus and checked in with the department and your sponsor, you MUST COMPLETE CHECK-IN AT OFFICE OF INTERNATIONAL SERVICES WITHIN <u>FIVE CALENDAR DAYS</u> but no later than the program beginning date on your I-20 under any circumstances.** Otherwise, your SEVIS record will be terminated and **YOU WILL FALL OUT OF STATUS.** During the check-in process, we will discuss some very important immigration matters relative to your stay at UTHSCSA and San Antonio.

On behalf of The University of Texas Health Science Center, we look forward to your arrival on our campus. I am enclosing some information that may be helpful to you as you prepare for your journey.

Sincerely,

Derek S. Yu
Director
Office of International Services

The University of Texas
Health Science Center at San Antonio
Mail Code 7819
7703 Floyd Curl Drive
San Antonio, Texas 78229-3900

Graduate School of Biomedical Sciences
Office of the Dean

(210) 567-3709
FAX: (210) 567-3719

November 2, 2007

Mr. Saurav Pathria
First Floor,Kothi No 6, Phase 4
Mohali, Punjab
India 160059

Dear Mr. Pathria:

Pursuant to your original letter of admission dated May 7, 2007, your admission into the Doctor of Philosophy degree program in Biochemistry at the Graduate School of Biomedical Sciences at The University of Texas Health Science Center at San Antonio has been deferred to the Spring 2008 semester.

Due to the timeframe involved, please stay in close contact with the Biochemistry program for specific ininformation regarding registration and orientation for the Spring 2008 semester.

As stated before, please remember that your admission is contingent on maintenance of a cumulative average of B or better through the last semester prior to your entry into graduate school.

As a student whose citizenship or permanent residence is outside of the United States, you will also be required to have the necessary visa and immigration status before admission can be authorized. The Office of International Services should be in contact with you regarding requirements and procedures.

It would be in your best interest to keep in contact with Dr. Neal Robinson, Committee on Graduate Studies Chair in the Biochemistry program, to properly prepare for your admission.

To inform us of your decision on this deferred acceptance, please complete the attached Statement of Intent and return it to us as soon as possible. You may electronically send it to stong@uthscsa.edu or fax it to (210) 567-3719.

Sincerely,

Merle S. Olson, Ph.D.   for Merle S. Olson
Dean

MSO/jms

cc: Neal Robinson, Ph.D., COGS Chair, Biochemistry
       Jean Jiang, Ph.D., Applicant Advisor, Biochemistry
       Registrar's Office
       Office of International Services

Mr. Saurav Pathria
First Floor, Kothi No 6, Phase 4
Mohali, Punjab
India 160059

STATEMENT OF INTENT

In order to facilitate your response to this offer of admission to the Graduate School of
Biomedical Sciences at The University of Texas Health Science Center at San Antonio,
please check one of the choices below, sign, date and return via e-mail or fax as
explained in your admissions letter.

Response Deadline: __AS SOON AS POSSIBLE_____

_____A.   I accept your offer of admission for the Spring semester of 2008.

_____B.   I decline your offer of admission for the Spring semester of 2008.

_____   _____
Signature   Date

Doctor of Philosophy in Biochemistry

e-mail: stong@uthscsa.edu
fax: (210) 567-3719

Print Form

The University of Texas Health Science Center at San Antonio
EXIT/CLEARANCE FORM
This form should be completed between the hours of 8:30 a.m.-4:30 p.m., Monday through Friday on your last work day.

SECTION I:
Name: Saurav Pathria   Dept: Biochemistry   Date 9/5/2012

Title Graduate Research Assistant   Employee ID#: 422831   Contact Phone #: (   )

Forwarding Address:

Purpose of Clearing: ☐Transfer ☑Termination ☐Retirement ☐Leave of Absence (specify):
**Transferring employees do not need to proceed to Human Resources. Return this form to your original department.

SECTION II:

Clearance Area	Location	University Property	Clearing Department Signature	N/A Initial
1. Employing Department		Computer, Phone, Software		xxxxxxxxxx
2. Library		Books, Journals, Bills		
3. University Police	Parking Services Office Rm. 1.343T	Permits, Keys, Badge		xxxxxxxxxx
4. Environmental Health & Safety	DTL School Rm. 1.346	Radioactive Materials/Devices Lab		xxxxxxxxxx
5. General Services	DTL School Rm. 2.500U,	Coats/Uniforms		
6. Institutional Review Board	DTL School 3rd Floor	Research (Human Subjects)		xxxxxxxxxx
7. Bursar-Cashier Window	MED School Rm. 113D	Corporate Card		xxxxxxxxxx
8. Lab Animal Resources	MED School Rm. 255A	Animals/Protocols		xxxxxxxxxx
9. Institutional Animal Care Pro.	MED School Rm. 400L	Animal/Protocols Research/Grant		xxxxxxxxxx
10. Grants Management	MED School	Accts.		xxxxxxxxxx

**Please visit inside.uthscsa.edu to deactivate HSC alert account

SECTION III: Human Resources/Benefits (ADM Bldg.)

Transfer to another state agency? ☐Yes ☐No   ☐Direct Deposit   ☐Semi-Monthly   ☐Lump Sum

☐Insurance (COBRA) ☐Sick Leave Pool ☐Retirement

Comments:

I certify that all appropriate areas have been properly cleared. I understand that The University of Texas Health Science Center at San Antonio reserves the right to request the restitution of or payment for any property or the settlement of any outstanding obligations that might have been excluded from this clearance process.

Employee
Signature: Date:

Witness: Date:

R: 6-11

Part 10. Your Signature With USCIS at the Time of Filing This Benefit Request

E-Signature Attestation

Benefit Seeker - I understand that submitting this benefit request and information does not in itself grant me any immigration status or any benefit. By my signature, I certify, swear or affirm, under penalty of perjury under the laws of the United States of America, that all information and evidence submitted to establish and maintain this account and to seek this benefit is true and correct. I authorize the release of any information from my records that the U.S. Citizenship and Immigration Services (USCIS) or another U.S. Federal agency should need at any time to determine eligibility for any immigration benefit, document, or service sought, including the Social Security Administration, Internal Revenue Service, Department of Justice, Department of State, Department of Labor, and any vital statistics bureau, licensing entity, or state benefit agency. By my signature, I acknowledge that I understand under section 262 of the Immigration and Nationality Act (INA), if I am an alien who has been or will be in the United States for more than 30 days, I am required to register with USCIS. I understand and acknowledge that, under section 265 of the INA, I am required to provide USCIS with my current physical address and written notice of any change of physical address within 10 days of the change. I understand that USCIS will use the most recent physical address that I provide for all future communications, including the service of a Notice to Appear, should USCIS need to initiate removal proceedings against me. I understand and acknowledge that if I change my physical address without written notice to USCIS, I will be held responsible for any communications sent to me at the most recent physical address that I provided to USCIS. Furthermore, I understand and acknowledge that if removal proceedings are initiated against me and I do not attend any hearing, including an initial hearing based on service of the Notice to Appear at the most recent physical address that I provided to USCIS or as otherwise provided by law, I may be ordered removed in my absence, and/or arrested by the Department of Homeland Security and removed from the United States.

Attorneys & Accredited Representatives - I understand that submitting this benefit request and information for my client does not in itself grant my client any immigration status or any benefit. By my signature, I certify, swear or affirm, under penalty of perjury under the laws of the United States of America, that all information and evidence submitted to establish and maintain this account and to seek this benefit is true and correct. I authorize the release of any information from my records that USCIS or another U.S. Federal agency should need at any time to determine my eligibility to access the online account services in USCIS ELIS.

USCIS Privacy Act Statement

AUTHORITIES: The information and associated evidence you provide is collected pursuant to the Immigration and Nationality Act of 1952 (P.I.. 82-414), as amended; the Homeland Security Act of 2002 (P.I.. 107-296); and Title 8 of the Code of Federal Regulations.

PURPOSE: The information that you submit may be used (1) to create or update your USCIS ELIS Account, (2) determine your eligibility for a requested benefit, which includes required national security and law enforcement checks, and/or (3) determine your eligibility to act as an attorney or accredited representative in USCIS ELIS.

ROUTINE USES: This information will be shared outside USCIS to assist in determining your eligibility to access the online account services, to file benefit requests on behalf of your clients, and/or to review your client's case status and in accordance with the approved routine uses described in the associated systems of records notices.

DISCLOSURE: The information you provide is voluntary. However, failure to provide accurate information may delay a final decision after submission of a benefit request or result in denial of any pending benefit requests. Please note that the system will record user information such as Internet Protocol Address and Web Browser type and version upon submission.

Electronically Signed by the:

Applicant

Full Name(First, Middle, Last):	*SAURAV PATHRIA*
Email Address:	*saurav_pathria@yahoo.com*
USCIS Account Identifier:	
IP Address:	*75.1.56.69*
eSignature Submission Date and Time:	*Sep 8, 2012 9:41:51 PM*
Browser Data:	*Mozilla/5.0 (Windows NT 6.1; WOW64) Apple WebKit/537.1 (KHTML, like Gecko) Chrome/21.0.1180.89 Safari/537.1*
USCIS Electronic Immigration System Session Identifier:	*rumAF_mYh92EeTv-L._A9EcB*

Note: *Your typed written full legal name submitted electronically as part of this document signifies you as the identified signatory. Any electronic filing with this method shall bind you as the signatory as if the document were physically signed and filed.*

www.ingramcontent.com/pod-product-compliance
Lightning Source LLC
Chambersburg PA
CBHW060148300526
45790CB00014B/375